30 M[inute...] 06282

KT-460-722

30 Minute Vegetarian Thai Cookbook

Sarah Beattie

Thorsons
An Imprint of HarperCollinsPublishers

Thorsons
An Imprint of HarperCollins*Publishers*
77–85 Fulham Palace Road,
Hammersmith, London W6 8JB

Published by Thorsons 1997
1 3 5 7 9 10 8 6 4 2

A catalogue record for this book
is available from the British Library

ISBN 0 7225 3425 6

Printed and bound in Great Britain by
Caledonian International Book Manufacturing Limited, Glasgow

Contents

B.C.F.T.C.S.
062822

Thank you to all who helped with this book, particularly Prasan (Khun Pip) Fargrajang of The Thai House Cookery School; The Foodland Diner and All Gaengs, Bangkok; the vendors at the night market, Hua Hin; Kim Thai Supermarket, Manchester; The Royal Thai Embassy, London; Wendy Coslett; Veronica Bailey and Dee Jardine at Farewise Travel; Donna and Kenny Sclater; Peter and Vivienne Hellens; *The Lonely Planet Guide to Thailand*; Jane Judd and Wanda Whiteley.

And most especially, much love and thanks to Michael Gray, Magdalena Gray and Dylan Beattie for their essential support and, as ever, discerning palates and constructive criticism.

Introduction

It is not surprising that Thai food has become so popular. Most dishes require minimal cooking, contain no dairy fats, are made with fresh ingredients and are full of flavour. Authentic Thai cooking takes time in preparation, but the recipes in this book are all designed to take you just 30 minutes or less. Traditionally Thais eat a number of dishes at each meal, the busy cook can choose to serve just one or two with rice or noodles for a complete and satisfying meal.

The actual cooking time, in most cases, is quite brief. It is useful to prepare all the ingredients first, laying them out on large plates, ready for final cooking. A good sharp knife will speed you on your way faster than any other single piece of equipment. Thais use a heavy chopper, which doubles as a garlic and chilli crusher and has a razor-sharp blade for effortlessly slicing vegetables. A tool that is a cross between a ladle and a fish slice is the most effective thing to use in the wok – it allows you to lift, stir, turn, crush and any other thing you might need to do. Thai woks have a flatter bottom than the Chinese ones we are used to. Simple steel woks are cheap and good – choose one with a wooden handle to make life easier. Also, ensure you have a metal cradle so that the wok will stand safely on your cooker. Food processors can be a boon – real Thai chefs won't hear of them, preferring to pound ingredients in granite mortars – use them for shredding, slicing, puréeing, mincing. Do stop to think though – sometimes a knife is quicker.

Thai flavours are balanced between sweet, sour, salty and spicy, either in the same dish or in the selection of dishes served together. Some combinations may seem strange, but set your prejudices aside and taste them before making up your mind.

Thais are very likely to decorate dishes before sending them to the table. Those in a hurry will not have time for the traditional delicate vegetable carving, but a last-minute sprinkle of basil, coriander (cilantro), finely chopped red chilli or shredded Kaffir lime leaves doesn't take long and makes all the difference to the look of a finished dish. It only takes five minutes to make some chilli or spring onion (scallion) flowers (see page 146).

The transliteration of Thai produces problems for the farang (foreigner). What is written by some as pad, can also appear as bhud, phad or phat. Gaeng can be kaeng, kang or gang. For this reason, a lot of the recipes in this book have been given descriptive English language names.

Stocking Up – Thai Ingredients

If you are going to enjoy cooking Thai food, you will need to add certain basic ingredients to your larder. Some of the items might require some seeking out, especially if you live outside the major cities. However, you can buy most in quantity, freezing some for later use. Some supermarkets are enterprisingly selling fresh Thai cooking packs, including lemongrass, coriander (cilantro), ginger and chillies.

Chillies

Thais use hundreds of fresh chillies, from the tiniest 'mouseshit' up to the great big prik yuak at 10 cm (5in) long. The truly tiny chillies are difficult to find outside Thailand, so the recipes here assume you are using the slightly larger 'bird' or 'birds' eye' chillies. Feel free to use more or less chilli according to your taste. Thais also use dried red chillies. These are used in Red Curry Paste (page 2) and the fresh ones are used in the even hotter Green Curry Paste (page 4). Coarsely ground red chilli powder is a very useful standby, as are commercially produced chilli-flavoured oil, pastes and bottled chillies. Always wash your hands after preparing chillies and keep your face away when you are grinding or chopping them.

Coconut Milk

It is as hard to imagine Thai cooking without the coconut as it is Mediterranean food without olive oil. See page 5 for how to make coconut milk. Alternatively, simply open a can!

Ginger

In Thailand, there are several gingery flavours – root ginger, galangal and krachai or lesser ginger. Each has a distinctive flavour. Root ginger is warm and spicy, galangal is slightly bitter and hot, while krachai is almost lemony. Due to availability, ginger may be the only option for you. Don't worry. Pick fat, heavy roots and store them wrapped in newspaper or in damp sand in a cool, dark place. You might find that it sprouts new pinkish lumps. Slice this young ginger finely and nibble it with salad. Prepared grated ginger is available in jars – as is garlic – which can be a great help, but watch out if you stir-fry it as it spits like mad.

Herbs

The herbs most commonly used in Thai cooking are basil and coriander (cilantro). Thais use three different sorts of basil, but, as we rarely have a choice, the recipes in this book simply state basil. If you are fortunate enough to find the smaller leaved holy basil, use it in those recipes where it is cooked (soups, curries, stir-fries). Both basil and coriander (cilantro) are used in large quantities. If you have the space, grow your own.

Lemongrass

Now becoming more widely available, lemongrass looks like a woody spring onion (scallion). It can be found fresh, dried or bottled.

You can freeze fresh stems if you shred them finely.

You can also grow your own on your bathroom or kitchen windowsill. Stand some stems in 5 mm (¼ in) water in the base of a jar. Check the water daily, topping up or rinsing as required. In a couple of weeks, roots will begin to sprout into the water. When the stems have a little root system each, pot them in a coir-based compost. Do not allow to them to become dried out, but do not waterlog them. In the summer months, you can keep the pots out of doors.

A powdered form of lemongrass – sereh – can also be used.

Kaffir Limes and Leaves
Another of those haunting citrusy notes in Thai cooking is provided by Kaffir lime leaves. If you find them, buy a big bunch and dry or freeze them for later use. They will keep a while with their branches in water and their glossy greenery makes a pleasing feature in the kitchen. The small hard Kaffir limes are used only for their rinds – they are very dry inside. The zest, though, is very aromatic. If you can't find any, use ordinary limes.

Pickles
You will find pickled or preserved vegetables in an Oriental store. Thais use the dry-salted radish and cabbage stems. These might sound unappetizing, but they are very savoury and add just the right 'bite'. They also use pickled garlic and other vegetables, stored in brine or a mixture of vinegar, sugar and salt.

Rice
The staple in Thailand, rice is eaten at virtually every meal. In fact, if someone asks you to dinner, they literally invite you to eat rice. Fragrant jasmine rice is now widely available, but if you cannot get it, you should use another good long-grain variety, such as basmati. Sticky rice, favoured in the North of Thailand,

must be soaked and then steamed. It is a time-consuming process and so it is not included in this book. Try it when you do have the time, though, as it is very good.

Rice flour is used in batters and noodles. Some noodles are also made with soya bean flour.

Soy Beans

The soy bean creeps into Thai food in a great many guises. Soy sauce is used, both the light and dark varieties (in this book it also takes the place of Thai fish sauce). If you can find it, mushroom soy sauce or mushroom ketchup will add an extra savoury note to your cooking. You can substitute salt for soy sauce if you prefer.

Beancurd (tofu) is Thailand's cheese. Use the firm, block variety – silken is not appropriate for Thai recipes. You may also find ready-fried cubes, this will save time in those recipes which require fried beancurd. Sticks of beancurd skins, like crumpled paper or corn husks, are available, dried, in packets. Red beancurd is a powerful-smelling, fermented product used for making sauces. Black bean and yellow bean sauces can be found in most supermarkets. They, too, are fermented and add depth and flavour to a dish.

Sugar

Thailand produces sugar cane and refined sugar, but more popular for cooking is palm sugar – nam tan peep – from the coconut or sugar palm tree. It has a lovely caramel flavour that is not unlike maple sugar. If you cannot find it, use light muscovado or brown sugar in its place.

Tamarind

Otherwise known as Indian date, the tamarind has a pleasant, sour taste. You can buy it in the form of a pulp – a gooey, dark brown paste – in plastic bags complete with seeds or as a processed bottled purée. The pulp must be soaked in hot water then rubbed through a sieve. If you are unable to find it, you can use some lemon or lime juice instead.

Tamarind leaves are used in Thai cooking, too, but they are very difficult to find so have not been included in the recipes in this book.

Basic Recipes

Red Curry Paste

Make this basic ingredient up in quantity and keep it in a clean, sealed jar in the refrigerator. Commercial varieties are available, but most contain shrimp, so read the label carefully if this matters to you.

To do this authentically, you would need a large granite mortar and pestle to pound the ingredients together. There is a slight loss of flavour using a blender to do the hard work for you, but not enough to fret about. An old-fashioned mincer (grinder) also gives good results.

The quantities given here will make approximately ten tablespoons of paste – enough for five curries. This paste is used to make Penang and yellow curries, too. If you become hooked on Thai food, you may like to double the quantities and make twice as much each time.

MAKES 10 TABLESPOONS

6	large dried red chillies, briefly soaked in warm water
115 g/4 oz/1 cup	peeled and quartered shallots
4	garlic cloves, crushed (minced)
2	teaspoons peeled and grated galangal or root ginger
15	black peppercorns
½	teaspoon coriander seeds
2	teaspoons salt
2	tablespoons chopped lemongrass

2 teaspoons grated zest of Kaffir lime or
an ordinary lime if unavailable

1) Place the chillies in a blender or food processor. Whizz until a paste forms.
2) Add the shallots, garlic and ginger and process again.
3) Add the lemongrass, ground salt and spices and lime zest to the chilli paste and blend again, briefly. Scrape into a clean, screw-topped jar, seal, store in the refrigerator and use within the next 3 to 4 weeks.

Cook's Notes
For Penang curries, add 2 whole star anise and 1 teaspoon cumin and substitute white peppercorns for black.

For yellow curries, add 1 tablespoon of mild Madras curry powder to the paste.

Green Curry Paste

The hottest of the Thai curries, green curries, are made using fresh chillies, not dried.

MAKES 1 SMALL JARFUL OF PASTE

20	small fresh red or green chillies, chopped
4	long fresh green chillies, deseeded and chopped
2	lemongrass stems, chopped
1 bunch	of spring onions (scallions), chopped
6	garlic cloves, crushed (minced)
4-cm/1½-in piece	of root ginger, peeled and chopped or
1 tablespoon	prepared ginger
	grated zest of a Kaffir lime or of an ordinary lime or lemon if unavailable
5	coriander (cilantro) roots, washed and chopped, if available
2 teaspoons	ground coriander
1 teaspoon	ground cumin
1 teaspoon	ground white pepper
2 teaspoons	salt

1) Process all the ingredients together in a blender or food processor until you have a smooth paste. Store in a clean, screw-topped jar in the refrigerator and use within 3 to 4 weeks.

Coconut Cream and Coconut Milk

Coconuts are used extensively in Thai food, in both sweet and savoury dishes. Making coconut milk and cream is a daily chore in most homes. Several ripe coconuts are halved and the white flesh is grated and then squeezed with water. The first 'pressing' makes the richer, fattier cream and the second makes the milk.

We can make coconut cream and milk in this same way, but it is very laborious and time-consuming. Supermarkets stock many different options for the busy cook:

- canned coconut milk – if you want coconut cream, don't shake the can, remove the top carefully and spoon off the thick top layer
- coconut cream in cartons – this is extra thick, so dilute with 240 ml/8 fl oz/1 cup warm water for cream and 570 ml/1 pint/ 2½ cups for coconut milk
- powdered coconut milk – follow the manufacturer's instructions
- creamed coconut – it looks like a bar of soap, but simply follow the manufacturer's instructions to reconstitute it
- desiccated (shredded) coconut – pour 285 ml/10 fl oz/1⅓ cups boiling water over 285 g/10 oz/3 cups desiccated (shredded) coconut, leave it to stand for 20 minutes, then squeeze it through muslin (cheesecloth). It now needs to be left to settle in order to skim off the 'cream'. This is the least satisfactory method and the most time-consuming.

Sauces

Nam Prik I

Strictly speaking Nam Prik, like so many other Thai dishes, should contain dried shrimps, but it is so flavourful that one does not feel their loss very much.

There are as many ways to make Nam Prik as there are elephants in Thailand, and just as many ways to serve it. The most common way to use it is as a sort of salad dressing or dip. Simply prepare a large plate of crudités – raw vegetables of all sorts, such as cauliflower and broccoli florets, carrot and celeriac (celery root) batons, cabbage and lettuce wedges, topped and tailed (trimmed) beans and mangetout (snow peas) – for an informal feast.

SERVES 4–6

6	small fresh green very hot Thai chillies
3	larger fresh green not very hot chillies (e.g., Anaheim)
2	medium red onions, peeled and quartered
4	medium ripe, flavoursome tomatoes
1	garlic bulb
1	medium aubergine (eggplant) or, if you can find them, 4 round green aubergines (eggplants)
	juice of 1 lime
2 tablespoons	soy sauce
1 teaspoon	sugar
½ teaspoon	salt

1) Preheat the oven to 230°C/450°F/Gas 8.
2) Put all the vegetables in a covered cast iron casserole and bake for 20 minutes, until tender.
3) Removing the stalks and the garlic peel, place all the vegetables in a blender or food processor. Blend them together with the lime juice, soy sauce, sugar and salt. Serve.

Nam Prik II

This Nam Prik is more 'jam-like' – use it almost like a chutney or relish.

SERVES 4–6

50 g/2 oz/¼ cup	garlic cloves
125 g/4½ oz/1 cup	peeled and trimmed shallots
75 g/2¾ oz/½ cup	fresh red medium hot chillies
3 tablespoons	vegetable oil
1 tablespoon	soy sauce
2 tablespoons	palm or light muscovado sugar
2 tablespoons	tamarind juice
½ teaspoon	salt

1) Grill (broil) the garlic, shallots and chillies, until softened.
2) Peel the garlic and remove the stalks from the chillies.
3) Reduce the vegetables to a paste in a blender or food processor, then fry the paste in the oil for 1–2 minutes.
4) Add the remaining ingredients and cook, stirring, for another 3 minutes. It can then be used straight away or left to cool, stored in a clean, screw-topped jar in the refrigerator and used within the next 2 to 3 weeks.

Red Chilli Sauce

This sauce doesn't take long to make, so you can make it on the spur of the moment to serve with crudités for a quick meal or with Deep-fried Eggs or Corncakes (pages 92 and 101). It will also keep in the refrigerator for two weeks or small amounts can be frozen.

MAKES 1 SMALL JARFUL OF SAUCE

16	large fresh red chillies, deseeded and chopped
4 tablespoons	lime juice
1 tablespoon	soft brown sugar
8	garlic cloves, crushed (minced)
2 tablespoons	soy sauce or mushroom ketchup
½ teaspoon	salt
250 ml/9 fl oz/generous cup	water
60 ml/2 fl oz/¼ cup	oil

1) Place all the ingredients in a small saucepan and bring slowly to the boil.
2) Simmer for 15 minutes, then process in a blender or food processor until smooth. Pour into a clean, screw-topped jar and seal to store.

Plum Sauce

A lovely sweet and sour sauce – you can omit the chillies if you prefer. You will find preserved plums at an oriental store or in larger supermarkets.

SERVES 4–6

3	preserved plums (see above)
3 tablespoons	rice vinegar
90 ml/3 fl oz/¹/₃ cup	water
4 tablespoons	sugar
3	small fresh chillies, thinly sliced

1) Pull the plums apart and remove the stones (pits).
2) Simmer the flesh in the vinegar and water for 5 minutes, mashing occasionally with a wooden spoon to break down the plums.
3) Stir in the sugar until it has dissolved, bring to the boil and cook for 2 minutes.
4) Add the chillies, then leave to cool before serving. If liked, transfer to a clean, screw-topped jar, store in the refrigerator and use within 1 to 2 weeks.

Ginger Sauce

Use this sauce with noodles or rice and vegetables.

SERVES 4–6

2 tablespoons	dried Chinese mushrooms (the broken pieces)
200 ml/7 fl oz/¾ cup	boiling water
3 tablespoons	chopped pickled ginger
3 tablespoons	chopped spring onions (scallions)
3 tablespoons	rice vinegar
3 tablespoons	palm or light muscovado sugar
2 tablespoons	dark soy sauce
1 tablespoon	cornflour (cornstarch)
2 tablespoons	cold water

1) Soak the mushrooms in the boiling water for 10 minutes.
2) Strain, saving the soaking liquor, and chop the mushrooms.
3) Put the mushrooms and liquor in a pan with the ginger, spring onions (scallions), vinegar, sugar and soy sauce and simmer for 5 minutes.
4) Mix the cornflour (cornstarch) with the cold water and stir into the sauce. Cook, stirring, until clear and thickened. Serve.

Chilli Pickle

A very useful standby to wake up simple dishes. Thais seem to eat it all the time. Instead of the usual Western sauce bottles on cheap cafe counters, you often see this pickle.

SERVES 4–6

2 tablespoons	light soy sauce
2 tablespoons	lime juice or rice vinegar
1 tablespoon	caster (granulated) sugar
6	small fresh chillies, thinly sliced

1) Just mix everything together in a small bowl and serve.

Salads

Som Tam

Green papaya makes Som Tam a tangy, lively salad. Most recipes call for the papaya to be pounded with the flavouring, which is obviously time-consuming and physically demanding. Some street vendors appear to sidestep this practice and their salad is still delicious, but, strictly speaking, not Som Tam as this name means pounded. Allow at least 15 minutes standing time before serving and this will let the flavours infuse somewhat.

SERVES 4–6

1	small, green papaya, peeled, deseeded and coarsely grated
50 g/2 oz/¼ cup	unroasted peanuts, roughly chopped
2	small fresh red chillies, thinly sliced into rounds
6	French or Kenya beans (fine green beans), cut into 1-cm/½-in pieces
2	garlic cloves, crushed (minced)
1	medium tomato, cut into slivers
	juice of 1 lime
2 tablespoons	light soy sauce
1 tablespoon	caster (granulated) sugar

1) Mix all the ingredients together very well and allow to stand, covered, in a cool place.

Cucumber Salad

If you prefer things a little less hot, use sweet red (bell) peppers instead of the chillies in this refreshing salad.

SERVES 4–6

2	large dried red chillies
3	garlic cloves
2 tablespoons	vinegar – rice or white wine
	good pinch of salt
2 tablespoons	palm or golden granulated sugar
1	large cucumber, thinly sliced
225 g/8 oz/2 cups	thinly sliced shallots or Spanish onions
2	large fresh red chillies, deseeded and thinly sliced

1) Pound or process the dried chillies and garlic to make a very coarse paste.
2) Put into a pan with the vinegar, salt and sugar. Heat, stirring, until the sugar dissolves, then boil for 2 minutes.
3) Toss together the cucumber, shallots or onions and fresh chillies and drizzle the hot dressing over. Allow to stand for about 15 minutes, then serve.

Bamboo Shoot Salad

SERVES 4–6

1	lettuce, leaves separated, washed and trimmed
2	garlic cloves, sliced
1	small fresh chilli, sliced
2 tablespoons	vegetable oil
125 g/4 oz/1 cup	leeks cut into fine strips
175 g/6 oz/¾ cup	shredded bamboo shoots
2 tablespoons	soy sauce
2 tablespoons	lime juice
1 tablespoon	sugar
85 g/3 oz/½ cup	sliced tomatoes

1) Line a plate with the lettuce leaves.
2) Fry the garlic and chilli in the oil until they are browning.
3) Add the leeks and stir-fry for 1 minute.
4) Add the bamboo shoots, soy sauce, lime juice and sugar. Toss about to mix well. Pile onto the lettuce and top with the tomatoes.

Simple Salad

Just as the name suggests, a very simple salad, but a delicious one that you will probably want to make quite often.

1	Iceberg lettuce, shredded
2	small fresh red chillies, finely chopped (minced)
½	cucumber, peeled and grated
2 tablespoons	chopped fresh coriander (cilantro)
	juice and finely grated zest of 1 lime
2 teaspoons	caster (granulated) sugar, optional

1) Mix all the ingredients together in a salad bowl and serve.

Carrot Som Tam

This is another version of the green papaya salad, Som Tam (page 16). Make both if you are feeding a crowd as the two different colours contrast well.

SERVES 4–6

1	Cos (Romaine) lettuce, separated into leaves, washed and trimmed
2	garlic cloves
3	fresh red chillies
2 tablespoons	roasted peanuts
3 tablespoons	lime juice
3 tablespoons	light soy sauce
2 tablespoons	sugar
50 g/2 oz/½ cup	chopped French beans (fine green beans)
250 g/9 oz/1½ cups	coarsely grated carrot

1) Spread the lettuce leaves out on a plate.
2) Whizz the garlic, chillies, peanuts, lime juice, soy sauce and sugar in a blender or food processor.
3) When they have combined, add the beans and whizz very briefly.
4) Transfer the mixture to a bowl, mix in the carrot well with a wooden spoon. Pile onto the lettuce and serve.

Spicy Mushroom Salad

Also known as Yam Hed (or Het) Hoo Noo, this could become Oh No if you are not wary about the amount of chilli.

Traditionally, such a salad is served with lettuce or cabbage leaves to scoop up mouthfuls of the spicy minced mushrooms.

SERVES 4–6

2 tablespoons	uncooked rice
225 g/8 oz/2 cups	mushrooms
1 tablespoon	vegetable oil
75 g/2¾ oz/½ cup	beancurd cut into thin strips
	juice of 1 lime
½–1 teaspoon	coarsely ground dried red chilli (add more if liked, but see above)
2 tablespoons	light soy sauce
2	shallots, finely chopped (minced)
2	spring onions (scallions), thinly sliced
15 g/½ oz/½ cup	roughly chopped fresh coriander (cilantro) leaves
7 g/¼ oz/½ cup	fresh mint leaves

1) Put the rice into a dry pan and shake over quite a high heat until the grains turn golden brown.
2) Whizz quickly in a blender or food processor or crush with a rolling pin until you have a coarse, bitty powder. Put to one side.
3) Mince the mushrooms with the oil in a food processor, using the pulse setting to chop them finely. Scrape into a pan and stir-fry until lightly browned. Remove with a slotted spoon.

4) In the same pan, fry the beancurd until lightly browned.
5) Mix together all the ingredients, except the mint leaves. Serve, garnishing with the mint leaves.

Cashew and Tomato Salad

SERVES 4–6

125 g/4 oz/1 cup	sliced celery sticks
1	small lettuce, separated into leaves, washed and trimmed
4	thin slices of ginger, finely chopped (minced)
2	garlic cloves, thinly sliced
1 tablespoon	vegetable oil
2	fresh mild red chillies, sliced on the diagonal to form ovals
1 teaspoon	fresh green peppercorns
4 tablespoons	unroasted cashews
2 tablespoons	soy sauce
1 teaspoon	palm or brown sugar
175 g/6 oz/1 cup	slightly under-ripe tomatoes, halved and sliced

1) Spread the celery and lettuce leaves out on a plate.
2) Fry the ginger and garlic in the oil until softening.
3) Add the chillies, green peppercorns and cashews. Stir-fry until the cashews are golden.
4) Add the soy sauce, sugar and tomatoes. Stir to just combine, then turn out onto the lettuce and celery and serve.

Chom Pu Yam

Chom pu are rose apples – fragrant, crisp and slightly tart when they are under-ripe, which is how you want them for this recipe. If you cannot find them, then use a good Granny Smith apple or some thinly sliced under-ripe babaco (star fruit).

SERVES 4–6

1	lettuce, separated into leaves, washed and trimmed
3	chom pu, thinly sliced
3	small fresh chillies, finely chopped (minced)
2	garlic cloves, thinly sliced
2 tablespoons	lime juice
2 tablespoons	light soy sauce
2 tablespoons	thinly sliced young ginger (page ix)
2	red onions, halved and thinly sliced
2 tablespoons	roughly chopped peanuts
1 tablespoon	sugar

1) Arrange the lettuce leaves on a plate.
2) Combine all the other ingredients, mixing well, and pile on top of the lettuce. Serve.

Curried Coconut Salad

This is a warm salad not a curry because the vegetables are barely cooked. It's not much of a distinction and should you overcook the vegetables, just serve it as a curry!

SERVES 4–6

400-ml/14-oz can	coconut milk
175 g/6 oz/2 cups	beansprouts
225-g/8-oz can	water chestnuts, drained and sliced
200 g/7 oz/1½ cups	sliced carrots
25 g/4½ oz/1 cup	celeriac (celery root) or celery sticks cut into batons
125 g/4½ oz/1½ cups	cut (into 2.5-cm/1-in pieces) yard-long or French beans (fine green beans)
125 g/4½ oz/2¼ cups	sliced Chinese cabbage
2 tablespoons	Red Curry Paste (page 2)
1 teaspoon	ground cumin
1 teaspoon	ground coriander
2 tablespoons	soy sauce
1 tablespoon	palm or soft brown sugar
75 g/2¾ oz/½ cup	peanuts briefly whizzed in a food processor or 2 tablespoons wholefood crunchy peanut butter (containing only peanuts)

1) Remove the thick cream from the coconut milk (page 5) and set aside. Pour the milk into a pan and add half a can of water. Bring to the boil and add the vegetables. Simmer for 3–4 minutes.

2) Drain, saving the coconut milk. Spread the vegetables out on a plate.

3) Heat the coconut cream until it separates.

4) Add the Red Curry Paste, cumin and coriander. Cook, stirring, for a minute. Stir in the soy sauce, sugar, peanuts and 4 tablespoons of the reserved coconut milk. Cook for 1 minute, stirring, then pour over the vegetables, toss and serve.

Shaddock Salad

Shaddock sounds like a fish but it is actually a fruit, similar to a grapefruit. It is also known as a pomelo or som oh in Thai. If you aren't keen on the bitter edge of shaddock or grapefruit, try using three ugli fruit instead.

SERVES 4–6

2	Little Gem (baby Romaine) lettuces, cut into rounds
2	shaddocks, peeled, segmented and pips (seeds) removed
3	large fresh mild red chillies, sliced
55-g/2-oz sachet	of creamed coconut
75 ml/3 fl oz/scant ½ cup	boiling water
3	garlic cloves, sliced
1 tablespoon	vegetable oil
1 tablespoon	Red Curry Paste (page 2)
1 tablespoon	light soy sauce
1 teaspoon	sugar
3 tablespoons	chopped peanuts

1) Line a plate with the lettuce. Cover with the shaddock and scatter the chillies over. Mix together the coconut and water.
2) Fry the garlic in the oil until crisp, then drain and reserve. Fry the Red Curry Paste in the same pan for 1 minute.
3) Add the soy sauce, sugar, peanuts and the coconut mixture. Mix well and allow to bubble. Pour over the salad and scatter on the garlic. Serve.

Mango Yam

A very exciting salad – sour, savoury, spicy and sweet, all zinging at once.

SERVES 4–6

1	medium, green mango, peeled and flesh sliced off stone (pit)
1 tablespoon	oil
2	garlic cloves, sliced
4	shallots, sliced
2	small fresh red chillies, sliced into rings
1 teaspoon	sliced young ginger (page ix)
1 tablespoon	light soy sauce
1 teaspoon	caster (granulated) sugar
1	lime, quartered

1) Cut the mango into matchsticks and place in a bowl.
2) Heat the oil and fry the garlic until nutty brown. Scoop it out with a slotted spoon and scatter over the mango. Do the same with the shallots and chillies.
3) Sprinkle the ginger, soy sauce and sugar over the salad. Mix well and serve with the quartered lime.

Khao Yam

This is a wonderful way to use leftover rice. If you don't have any, either resort to using tinned rice or cook some and then run it under cold water as soon as it is cooked. Drain then pat it dry in a clean tea towel (dish cloth)-lined colander.

SERVES 4–6

2 tablespoons	desiccated (shredded) coconut
1 teaspoon	sugar
340 g/12 oz/2¼ cups	cooked rice
2 stems	young lemongrass, shredded
1 tablespoon	young ginger, peeled and cut into matchsticks
4	spring onions (scallions), green and white parts separated and thinly sliced
2	yard-long or French beans (fine green beans) cut into 1-cm/½-in pieces
85 g/3 oz/½ cup	grated (shredded) carrot
85 g/3 oz/½ cup	grated (shredded) mooli
75 g/2¾ oz/½ cup	chopped roasted cashews

SAUCE

2 tablespoons	soft brown sugar
4 tablespoons	rice vinegar
3–4	small fresh chillies, sliced

1) Mix together the coconut and sugar and heat gently, stirring, in a wok. Do not put them into an already hot wok as the sugar would burn straight away. Cook until a lovely toasted brown. Remove from the wok and allow to cool.

2) Mound the rice on a large plate and surround with neat piles of lemongrass, ginger, spring onions, beans, carrot, mooli, cashews and coconut.

3) Make the sauce by dissolving the sugar in the vinegar and stirring in the sliced chilli. Diners help themselves to a spoonful of rice and combine it with whatever selection of accompaniments they want. Serve the chilli sauce separately to dribble over.

Aubergine (Eggplant) Yam

The similarity of this dish to Middle Eastern ones is startling. In fact, you could cheat by buying tinned Baba Ghanoush, adding soy sauce, chillies, lime zest and juice and coriander (cilantro) – not quite the same, but still delicious and extremely quick.

SERVES 4–6

1	long, slender aubergine (eggplant) (up to 340 g/12 oz)
4	small fresh chillies, chopped
1	Spanish (mild) onion, finely chopped (minced)
2 tablespoons	chopped Chinese chives or the green part of a spring onion (scallion) if unavailable
2 teaspoons	caster (granulated) sugar
	juice and finely grated zest of 1 lime
2 tablespoons	mushroom soy or light soy sauce
15 g/½ oz/½ cup	sprigs of fresh coriander (cilantro)

1) Grill (broil) the aubergine (eggplant) until the skin has blackened and the flesh softened.
2) Scrape off the skin and cut the flesh into rounds, laying them out on a plate.
3) Mix together the remaining ingredients, except the coriander (cilantro), and spoon over the aubergine (eggplant) slices.
4) Garnish with the coriander (cilantro) and serve.

Soups

Tom Yam Het

Tom means boiled, yam means together and het are mushrooms – this is a clear Thai mushroom soup. Ideally, it is made using straw mushrooms, but if these are unavailable, use tightly closed button or chestnut mushrooms instead.

SERVES 4–6

1 litre/1¾ pints/4 cups	water
4 thin slices	of galangal or fresh root ginger if unavailable
1 tablespoon	chopped lemongrass
4	Kaffir lime leaves, roughly torn
115 g/4 oz/1 cup	chopped shallots or Spanish onion
100 ml/3½ fl oz/½ cup	mushroom ketchup or light soy sauce
225 g/8 oz/2 cups	mushrooms
115 g/4 oz/1 cup	baby sweetcorn cut into 2.5-cm/1-in lengths
100 ml/3½ fl oz/½ cup	lime juice
3	small fresh chillies
handful	of fresh coriander (cilantro)

1) Bring the water to the boil.
2) Add the galangal or ginger, lemongrass, lime leaves and shallots or onions. Stir and bring back to the boil.
3) Add the mushroom ketchup or soy sauce, mushrooms and sweetcorn. Simmer for 5 minutes.
4) Stir in the lime juice. Crush the chillies with the flat of a knife, then roughly chop and throw them in.
5) Break the coriander (cilantro) stem into 5-cm/2-in lengths, add to the soup, stir through and serve hot.

Tom Kha Het

This is a creamy mushroom soup, but very unlike the Western cream of mushroom soups you may be used to. At the Foodland Diner in Bangkok, it is served fiery hot – too hot for me – with optional extra chilli to sprinkle over!

SERVES 4–6

400-ml/14-oz can	coconut milk
715 ml/1¼ pints/3 cups	warm water
450 g/1 lb/4 cups	mushrooms
2.5-cm/1-in piece	of young galangal, finely sliced, or 2 teaspoons grated root ginger if unavailable
1 tablespoon	shredded lemongrass
4	Kaffir lime leaves, rolled up tightly and finely sliced
100 ml/3½ fl oz/¹/₃ cup	light soy sauce
100ml/3½ fl oz/¹/₃ cup	lime juice
handful	of fresh coriander (cilantro), roughly chopped
3	fresh chillies, crushed and chopped

1) Shake the can of coconut milk before opening, then pour all but 125 ml/4 fl oz/½ cup into a pan.
2) Add the warm water and stir.
3) Add the mushrooms, galangal or root ginger, lemongrass and lime leaf shreds. Bring to the boil, then simmer for 5 minutes.
4) Add the soy sauce and the reserved coconut milk. Bring back to the boil, then take off the heat, add the lime juice, coriander (cilantro) and chillies and serve.

Egg Noodle Soup

Fresh vegetable stock is available in most supermarkets if you haven't any home-made. Other possibilities, in descending order of preference, can be stock made using Japanese miso paste, vegetable bouillon powder and vegetable stock (bouillon) cubes.

SERVES 4–6

1 litre/1¾ pints/4 cups	stock (see above)
125 g/4 oz/1 cup	cut (into 1-cm/½-in pieces) yard-long or runner beans
1 tablespoon	palm or brown sugar
2 tablespoons	mushroom ketchup
4 tablespoons	dark soy sauce
125 g/4 oz	ba mee (dried egg noodles), soaked and drained
4	fresh chillies, finely sliced
75 g/2¾ oz/½ cup	chopped roasted peanuts
125 g/4½ oz/1½ cups	beansprouts

1) Bring the stock to the boil and cook the beans in it for 1 minute.
2) Stir in the sugar, ketchup and soy sauce.
3) In the bottom of each soup dish, place a pile of noodles, top with some chillies, peanuts and beansprouts. Ladle the stock and beans over and serve.

Beancurd Soup

Ready-made Italian gnocchi take the place here of the fish balls in the Thai original. They have the same floury texture, are widely available and are vegetarian.

SERVES 4–6

570 ml/1 pint/2½ cups	vegetable stock (page 36)
1 tablespoon	pickled radish, chopped, or 1 teaspoon grated lime zest if unavailable
2 tablespoons	mushroom ketchup or an extra 2 tablespoons soy sauce if unavailable
1 tablespoon	soy sauce
1 stem	lemongrass, finely sliced
175 g/6 oz/1 cup	ready-made Italian gnocchi
125 g/4 oz/¾ cup	cubed firm beancurd
30 g/1 oz/¼ cup	chopped spring onions (scallions)
2	small fresh red chillies, finely chopped (minced)

1) Put the stock, pickled radish or lime zest, mushroom ketchup or extra soy sauce, soy sauce and lemongrass into a pan and bring to the boil.

2) Reduce to a simmer and add the gnocchi. Cook for 3 minutes.

3) Add the beancurd and cook for a further 3 minutes.

4) Then, add the spring onions (scallions) and chillies. Cook for 1 minute more, then serve.

Rice Soup

Leftover rice is always useful and here's an excellent use for it. If you haven't any cooked rice to hand but want to try out this soup (Thais claim its efficacy as a hangover cure can't be bettered), then use the tinned microwaveable rice for speed.

SERVES 4–6

55 g/2 oz/½ cup	oyster mushrooms, thinly sliced
0.5 litre/18 fl oz/2 cups	vegetable stock (page 36)
2 tablespoons	light soy sauce
good pinch	of finely chopped pickled radish
good pinch	of white pepper
255 g/9 oz/1½ cups	cooked or canned rice
2	garlic cloves, thinly sliced or, if feeling more robust, 1 small fresh green chilli, thinly sliced
2 tablespoons	oil

1) Put the oyster mushrooms, stock, soy sauce, pickled radish and pepper into a pan and bring to the boil, then simmer for 4 minutes.
2) Stir in the rice and cook for a further 5–7 minutes (the longer time if you are using canned rice).
3) Meanwhile, fry the garlic or chilli in the oil. Add a spoonful of the garlicky oil to each bowl of soup.

Tom Fak

Pumpkin soup as the Pilgrim Fathers never imagined it!

SERVES 4–6

1 litre/1¾ pints/4 cups	vegetable stock (page 36)
2	Kaffir lime leaves
1 tablespoon	finely shredded lemongrass
2 tablespoons	light soy sauce
1 tablespoon	palm or brown sugar
2 teaspoons	Red Curry Paste (page 2)
370 g/13 oz/3 cups	cubed pumpkin

1) Put everything into a pan. Bring to the boil and simmer for about 10–15 minutes, until the pumpkin is just tender. Serve.

Soy and Vermicelli Soup with Carrot Flowers

Carrot flowers are so simple to make and so effective. Just cut five V-shaped grooves along the length of the carrot then slice cross wise.

SERVES 4–6

4	garlic cloves, crushed (minced)
1	medium onion, finely chopped (minced)
1 tablespoon	vegetable oil
1 teaspoon	shredded lemongrass
8	thin slices of ginger, cut into slivers
1 tablespoon	palm or brown sugar
4 tablespoons	dark soy sauce
0.5 litre/18 fl oz/2 cups	water
1	carrot, prepared as given above
55 g/2 oz	rice vermicelli, soaked and drained

1) Fry the garlic and onion in the oil until golden.
2) Add all the other ingredients, apart from the vermicelli. Simmer for 5 minutes.
3) Divide the vermicelli between small (cup-sized) soup bowls and ladle the soup over it.

Curries

Mushroom and Bamboo Shoots in Red Curry

Fresh bamboo shoots are almost unheard of outside the East. This dish therefore uses the canned variety. It also uses canned straw mushrooms, prepared pastes and coconut milk, so it is the ideal 'unexpected guest' meal as virtually all the ingredients come off the shelves in the cupboard.

SERVES 4–6

225-g/8-oz can	straw mushrooms
140 g/5 oz/²/₃ cup	canned bamboo shoots, rinsed, drained and shredded
225-g/8-oz can	baby sweetcorn, rinsed and drained
1 tablespoon	Red Curry Paste (page 2)
400-ml/14-oz can	coconut milk
125 ml/4½ fl oz/½ cup	water
2 tablespoons	light soy sauce
2 teaspoons	palm or brown sugar
3	Kaffir lime leaves, shredded
2	fresh red chillies, thinly sliced
15 g/½ oz/½ cup	fresh basil leaves

1) Put the mushrooms, bamboo shoots, baby sweetcorn, Red Curry Paste, coconut milk, water, soy sauce and sugar into a pan and bring to the boil, stirring. Simmer for 7 minutes.

2) Add the lime leaves, chillies and basil. Serve.

Green Green Curry

Doubly green due to the vegetables, this curry uses the hotter fresh chilli paste, the recipe for which is on page 4, or else you can buy some ready-made.

SERVES 4–6

1½ 400-ml/14-oz cans	coconut milk
3 tablespoons	Green Curry Paste (page 4)
225 g/8 oz/1½ cups	trimmed and cut (into 5-cm/2-in lengths) spring onions (scallions)
225 g/8 oz/4 cups	broccoli florets
125 g/4 oz/1½ cups	cut (into 5-cm/2-in lengths) French or Kenya beans (fine green beans)
125 g/4 oz/1 cup	cut (into strips 5-cm/2-in long) courgettes (zucchini)
4	Kaffir lime leaves, torn
3 teaspoons	light soy sauce
2 teaspoons	palm or soft brown sugar
30 g/1 oz/1 cup	fresh basil leaves
2	small fresh red chillies, finely sliced

1) Open the can of coconut milk without shaking it first, spoon off the thick coconut cream and put it into a hot wok. Bring to the boil, stirring. (Set the can with the remaining milk to one side.)
2) Add the Green Curry Paste and cook, stirring, for 2 minutes.
3) Add the vegetables and stir well.
4) Pour in the remaining coconut milk and 1 canful of warm water.

5) Add the lime leaves, soy sauce and palm sugar and simmer for about 10 minutes, until the vegetables are tender.
6) Scatter the basil leaves and chillies over the top. Serve.

Green Curry with Beancurd

Beancurd, or tofu, is used frequently in Thailand. Great blocks of the pressed soya bean curds sit glistening wetly in the market. High in protein, low in fat, it is *the* health food. Its drawback is that it has no flavour of its own. However, in this green curry, it becomes very tasty indeed.

SERVES 4–6

400-ml/14-oz can	coconut milk
3 tablespoons	Green Curry Paste (page 4)
340 ml/12 fl oz/1½ cups	vegetable stock
140 g/5 oz/1 cup	sliced carrots
225 g/8 oz/2 cups	sliced oyster mushrooms
1 bunch	of watercress, washed and trimmed
255 g/9 oz/1½ cups	cubed firm beancurd
3 tablespoons	light soy sauce
1 tablespoon	palm sugar or light muscovado
1 tablespoon	green peppercorns in brine, rinsed and drained
2	fresh red chillies, finely sliced
30 g/1 oz/1 cup	torn fresh basil leaves

1) Open the can of coconut milk without shaking it first, spoon off the thick coconut cream and put it into a hot wok. Bring to the boil, stirring. (Set the can with the remaining milk to one side.)
2) As it begins to separate, add the Green Curry Paste. Stir-fry for 1 minute.
3) Add the remaining coconut milk, the stock, carrots and mushrooms. Cook for 2 minutes.

4) Add the watercress, beancurd, soy sauce and sugar. Cook for a further 4 minutes.
5) Stir in the green peppercorns, chillies and basil. Serve.

Mussaman Curry

Mussaman is the Thai word for Muslim and it is used for curries with a more Malay/Indian flavour that have been introduced from the South.

Use the biggest, darkest mushrooms you can find – about 10-cm/4-in diameter ones.

SERVES 4–6

4	cardamom pods
1 teaspoon	cumin seeds
2	bay leaves
½ teaspoon	ground cinnamon
½ teaspoon	ground cloves
60 ml/2 fl oz/¼ cup	vegetable oil
3	garlic cloves, peeled and sliced
2	medium red onions, trimmed, leaving a little of the root, and cut into eighths (like orange segments)
4	medium waxy potatoes, peeled and cut into eighths
4	very large flat mushrooms, cubed
3 tablespoons	Red Curry Paste (page 2)
400-ml/14-oz can	coconut milk
60 ml/2 fl oz/¼ cup	tamarind purée
4 tablespoons	rich dark soy sauce
2 tablespoons	palm or soft brown sugar
150 g/5½ oz/1 cup	roasted peanuts

1) Heat a wok and dry roast the cardamom pods, cumin seeds and bay leaves for 1 minute.
2) Add the ground spices and remove from the heat.
3) Crush in a spice mill or tip into a clean envelope and pulverize with a rolling pin.
4) Heat half the oil in the wok and fry the garlic, onions and potatoes until browning.
5) Remove with a slotted spoon.
6) Fry the mushrooms. Drain and add to the potatoes and onions.
7) Fry the Red Curry Paste with the ground spices in the remaining oil, add the vegetables back in, mixing well. Add half the coconut milk and all the tamarind, soy sauce and sugar. Simmer.
8) Meanwhile, put the peanuts into a blender or food processor. After a short burst, remove half the peanuts. Process the remainder until they are finely ground. Scrape into the curry, add the coarsely chopped peanuts and the remaining coconut milk. Simmer until the potatoes are quite tender. Serve.

Christophene Curry

Christophenes have many aliases. You will find them also called chayote, cho-cho, chow-chow and vegetable pear. They originally came from Central America but their use has spread to South-East Asia. If you cannot find any, vegetable marrows are a reasonable substitute.

SERVES 4–6

400-ml/14-oz can	coconut milk
400 ml/14 fl oz/1¾ cups	water
2	Christophenes, cubed
150 g/5 oz/1 cup	thickly sliced carrots
85 g/3 oz/1 cup	cut (into 2.5-cm/1-in lengths) baby sweetcorn
2 tablespoons	Green Curry Paste (page 4)
3	Kaffir lime leaves, torn
2 teaspoons	palm or light muscovado sugar
3 tablespoons	soy sauce
20 g/¾ oz/¾ cup	fresh basil leaves
2	fresh red chillies, finely sliced

1) Open the can of coconut milk, without shaking it first, and spoon out the thick cream, reserving it for later. Pour the remaining milk into a wok with the water and bring to the boil.
2) Add the vegetables and cook for about 10 minutes, until the milk has reduced and the vegetables are just tender.
3) Tip into a bowl. Wipe the wok.
4) Heat the wok, then add the coconut cream. Cook, stirring, for 1 minute.

5) Add the Green Curry Paste. Using a slotted spoon, add in the vegetables and the lime leaves.
6) Stir in the sugar and soy sauce. Add the coconut milk left in the bowl, the basil and chillies. Serve.

Sweet Potato Penang

This fragrant curry can also be made with parsnips or large, old carrots.

SERVES 4–6

400-ml/14-oz can	coconut milk
3 tablespoons	Penang Curry Paste (see under Red Curry Paste, page 3)
1 kg/2 lbs 4 oz/7 cups	peeled and cut (into 4-cm/1½-in chunks) sweet potatoes
125 g/4½ oz/1½ cups	cut (into 5-cm/2-in lengths) Kenya or French beans (fine green beans)
6	Kaffir lime leaves, torn
2 tablespoons	mushroom ketchup or light soy sauce
1 tablespoon	palm or brown sugar
55 g/2 oz/⅓ cup	coarsely chopped roasted cashews or peanuts
2	small fresh red chillies, finely sliced
a handful	of fresh sweet basil

1) Open the can of coconut milk without shaking it first. Spoon out half of the contents into a wok and reduce by half over a fairly high heat, stirring from time to time. Remove 1 tablespoon of the thickened cream and reserve.
2) Stir in the Penang Curry Paste and cook, stirring, for 4 minutes.
3) Add the sweet potatoes and stir until all are coated.
4) Add the beans.
5) Mix the remainder of the can of coconut milk with a can and a half of warm water. Add to the wok with the Kaffir lime

leaves and the mushroom ketchup or soy sauce. Simmer for about 10–15 minutes, until the sweet potatoes are just tender.

6) Stir in the sugar, nuts, chillies and basil. Serve topped with the reserved thickened coconut cream.

Rice

Plain Rice

If you have your own favourite way of cooking rice that never fails, skip this page. If, however, your rice is never right, read on. There are lots of different ways to produce perfect rice and expensive electric rice cookers to help you, too, but a cup and a good saucepan with a tight-fitting lid are all you need.

SERVES 1–2
1 cupful of Thai jasmine (fragrant) rice
1½ cupfuls of boiling water

1) Rinse the rice, then drain it.
2) Put the rice into a saucepan and pour on the boiling water. Stir it around as it comes back to the boil. Then, turn the heat down until the water is barely simmering, cover the pan tightly and leave to cook for 10 minutes.
3) Turn off the heat, but leave, covered, for 5 minutes.
4) Fluff the rice up with a fork and serve.

Cook's Note
You can add subtle extra flavours by popping some lime leaves or a stick of lemongrass in with the rice while it is cooking. Discard the leaves or lemongrass before serving.

Curried Rice

This wonderful, yellow, garlicky rice makes a great accompaniment to many different stir-fries, but double the quantities and use half the next day in a fried rice dish or in Khao Yam (page 29).

SERVES 4–6

6	garlic cloves, crushed (minced)
2 tablespoons	vegetable oil
300 g/10½ oz/1½ cups	long-grain rice
1 teaspoon	Madras curry powder
1 teaspoon	salt
800 ml/1½ pints/3¾ cups	boiling water or stock

1) Fry the garlic in the oil in a heavy based pan with a tight-fitting lid until golden.
2) Stir in the rice and fry for 1 minute longer.
3) Add the curry powder and salt. Mix well, then pour on the water or stock. Stir, cover, turn the heat down until it is barely simmering and cook for 13 minutes – do not remove the lid.
4) Allow the rice to stand, covered, for 5 minutes. Fluff with a fork and serve.

Fried Rice and Vegetables

This is simplicity itself, using some leftover rice and a few vegetables. Vary the vegetables according to what you have to hand – those given in the recipe are merely suggestions. Season to taste with a light soy sauce or salt. Add a fried egg per person if desired.

SERVES 4–6

2 tablespoons	vegetable oil
200 g/7 oz/1½ cups	mixed prepared vegetables (e.g., fine asparagus or French beans (fine green beans), slivers of tomato, sliced broccoli or greens' stems, tiny baby sweetcorn, oyster mushrooms)
450 g/1 lb/3 cups	cooked Plain Rice (page 54)

1) Heat the oil in a wok. Fry the vegetables quickly, stirring all the time.
2) Stir in the rice and heat through, tossing like a salad. Serve.

Fried Rice II

Slightly more involved than Fried Rice and Vegetables (page 56), but this is still quick and easy fried rice. It is Khao Pad Khai in Thai, egg-fried rice.

SERVES 4–6

2 tablespoons	vegetable oil
2	garlic cloves, sliced
1–2	fresh chillies, finely chopped
225 g/8 oz/2 cups	quartered (unless small, then leave whole) closed cap mushrooms
3 tablespoons	soy sauce
1 tablespoon	palm or light brown sugar
a handful	of fresh basil leaves
340 g/12 oz/2 cups	cooked rice
2	eggs
1	small fresh mild red chilli, diced
1	small onion, diced

1) Heat the oil in a wok. Fry the garlic until brown.
2) Add the chillies. Stir-fry for 30 seconds, then add the mush-rooms. Stir-fry for 1 minute.
3) Add the soy sauce and sugar. Throw in the basil leaves. Toss around.
4) Stir in the rice.
5) Push the rice to the edges of the wok and crack in the eggs. Lightly scramble, allow to set slightly, then mix into the rice.
6) Sprinkle in the mild chilli and onion, mix and serve immediately.

Red Beans and Fried Rice

Not Louisiana red beans, this is fermented beancurd and is to be found canned or in earthenware pots in oriental stores.

SERVES 4–6

2	garlic cloves, crushed (minced)
2 tablespoons	vegetable oil
170 g/6 oz/1½ cups	courgettes (zucchini) cut into strips
3 tablespoons	dark soy sauce
2	eggs
1 tablespoon	palm or soft brown sugar
450 g/1 lb/3 cups	cooked rice
a handful	of fresh coriander (cilantro), chopped
4	shallots, finely chopped (minced)
2 teaspoons	grated fresh root ginger
4	small fresh red chillies, finely chopped (minced)
85 g/3 oz /½ cup	mashed red beancurd (see above)
	juice of 1 lime

1) Fry the garlic in the oil until golden.
2) Add the courgettes (zucchini) and stir-fry for 1 minute.
3) Add the soy sauce. Break in the eggs. As they begin to set, mix around.
4) Add the sugar and rice. Stir-fry for 4 minutes.
5) Add the coriander (cilantro) and 1 tablespoon of the shallots.
6) Mix together the rest of the shallots, the ginger, chillies and red beancurd. Thin with the lime juice to make a sauce and serve with the fried rice.

Coconut Rice

One of the easiest ways to make coconut rice is to add desiccated (shredded) coconut to the dry rice before cooking (allow 25 g/ 1 oz/^{1}/$_3$ cup to each 200 g/7 oz/1 cup of rice). However, the following recipe gives superior results.

SERVES 4–6

2	garlic cloves, crushed (minced)
2 tablespoons	vegetable oil
340 g/12 oz/2^1/$_4$ cups	just cooked rice
55-g/2-oz sachet	of creamed coconut
2 tablespoons	boiling water

1) Fry the garlic in the oil until golden.
2) Add the rice, stir-frying briefly.
3) Mix the creamed coconut with the boiling water, then add this to the rice and combine well. Serve.

Noodles

Curried Soft-fried Noodles

Almost as quick as pot-noodles but so much nicer.

SERVES 4–6

60 ml/2 fl oz/¼ cup	vegetable oil
2–3	garlic cloves, peeled and thinly sliced
1 tablespoon	Red Curry Paste (page 2)
170 g/6 oz/2 cups	thinly sliced closed cap mushrooms
115 g/4 oz/1 cup	courgettes (zucchini) cut into 5-cm/2-in strips
200 g/7 oz	noodles (egg thread or rice vermicelli), soaked and drained
2 tablespoons	light soy sauce
1 tablespoon	mushroom ketchup
1 teaspoon	sugar

1) Heat the oil in a wok. Fry the garlic slices until golden.
2) Add the Red Curry Paste – stand back, it will spit.
3) Stir in the mushrooms. Fry for 1 minute.
4) Add the courgettes (zucchini). Stir around.
5) Add the noodles and the remaining ingredients. Continue to cook, stirring, until the noodles are done – about 2–3 minutes. Serve.

Pad Thai

Pad Thai – noodles with egg – is almost a national dish, but, like Irish stew, everyone swears that their way of making it is the *only* way to do it. Therefore, I have chosen my two favourite ways of making Pad Thai (vegetarian-style, of course).

SERVES 4–6

2 tablespoons	vegetable oil
2	garlic cloves, chopped
170 g/6 oz	thin rice noodles, soaked in boiling water, then drained
1	large (extra large) egg
2 tablespoons	soy sauce
good pinch	of sugar
75 g/2¾ oz/¹⁄₃ cup	sliced fried firm beancurd
1 tablespoon	chopped pickled radish or turnip
2 tablespoons	chopped peanuts
85 g/3 oz/1 cup	beansprouts
1 tablespoon	chopped fresh coriander (cilantro)
1	lime, cut into wedges

1) Heat the oil in a wok. Fry the garlic until browning. Add the noodles. Fry them lightly, then push them to the sides of the wok.
2) Break in the egg. Gently mix it up in the base of the wok. As it begins to set, turn it over and break it up, mixing it into the noodles.
3) Mix in all the other ingredients in turn and serve, garnished with a few wedges of lime.

Pad Thai II – Noodles with Egg II

This is a slightly more involved version of Pad Thai (page 63), but it is still quick to make and even more delicious.

SERVES 4–6

115 ml/4 fl oz/½ cup	vegetable oil
3	shallots, chopped
3	garlic cloves, chopped
100 g/3½ oz/scant cup	sliced oyster mushrooms
3 tablespoons	chopped pickled radish
140 g/5 oz/¾ cup	firm beancurd cut into strips
1 teaspoon	coarsely ground dried red chillies
300 g/10½ oz	thin flat rice noodles, soaked and drained
60 ml/2 fl oz/¼ cup	tamarind water (page xi)
3	eggs
3 tablespoons	light soy sauce
2 tablespoons	palm or light muscovado sugar
1 tablespoon	chopped spring onion (scallion)
1 tablespoon	chopped fresh coriander (cilantro)
100 g/3½ oz/¾ cup	coarsely ground peanuts

1) Heat 3 tablespoons of the oil in a wok. Stir-fry the shallots and garlic until just golden.

2) Add the oyster mushrooms, then the pickled radish, beancurd and ground dried chillies, stirring well after each addition. Tip into a bowl.

3) Heat another 3 tablespoons of the oil. When it is hot, add the noodles and tamarind juice. Keep them on the move to prevent sticking. Cook for 3 minutes.

4) Mix the noodles in with the mushroom mixture.

5) Heat the remaining oil in the wok and add the eggs, spreading them thinly up the sides. When the eggs have set, chop them up and mix in the noodles and mushrooms.

6) Add the soy sauce and sugar. Stir until the sugar has melted.

7) Sprinkle the spring onion (scallion), coriander (cilantro) and peanuts over the top and mix lightly. Serve.

Soy Noodles and Courgettes (Zucchini)

Wonderfully savoury, double these quantities and serve on its own as a superfast supper.

SERVES 4–6

2	garlic cloves, sliced
2	small fresh chillies, chopped
2 tablespoons	vegetable oil
100 g/3½ oz/1 cup	sliced mushrooms
2	small courgettes (zucchinis), sliced into thin strips, lengthwise
100 g/3½ oz/1 cup	beansprouts
75 g/2¾ oz/½ cup	roasted cashews
4 tablespoons	dark soy sauce
100 g/3½ oz	egg noodles, soaked and drained

1) Fry the garlic and chillies in the oil for a few seconds.
2) Add the mushrooms and courgettes (zucchini) and stir-fry for 1 minute.
3) Add the beansprouts and cashews. Fry for a further minute.
4) Add the soy sauce and noodles. Stir-fry a further 2 minutes. Serve.

Crispy Noodles

These light, crisp noodles are a delicious accompaniment or dust them with chilli powder and salt for an unauthentic but very moreish nibble to snack on with beer.

SERVES 4–6

oil, for deep-frying

good handful of sen lek noodles (medium ribbon rice noodles)

1) Heat the oil to 365°F/185°C.
2) Drop in some noodles. They will immediately twist and writhe in the oil, puffing slightly. With two slotted spoons, turn the noodles, carefully making sure they are evenly puffed. Remove and drain on kitchen paper. Fry the rest, drain and serve.

Cook's Note
Any unpuffed bits will be tough and leathery, so be vigilant and turn each piece.

Crispy Noodles II

This is a complete dish rather than just an accompaniment. Known as Meeh Grob or Mee Krop, it is sweetish. It is relatively quick to make if you keep two pans on the heat at once, which is not difficult.

SERVES 4–6

	oil, for deep-frying
140 g/5 oz	sen mee (thin rice vermicelli)
1	large egg, beaten
1	red onion, halved and sliced
3	garlic cloves, sliced
85 g/3 oz/1 cup	sliced mushrooms
2 tablespoons	light soy sauce
2 tablespoons	tamarind water (page xi)
2 tablespoons	palm or light muscovado sugar
1 tablespoon	dark soy sauce
2 tablespoons	water or vegetable stock, if you have some
1	large fresh medium-hot red chilli, cut into slivers
1 tablespoon	chopped Chinese chives or spring onion (scallion) if unavailable

1) In a pan, heat some oil for deep-frying. When it is 375°F/190°C, drop in small batches of the sen mee. It will puff up and begin to turn golden in a matter of seconds. Fry all the vermicelli until it is crisp and lightly golden.

2) Carefully pour a little of the hot oil into another pan, then pour away all but 2 tablespoons of the rest of the oil.

3) In the second pan, fry the egg in a thin omelette until set, remove and slice into strips.

4) In the first pan, stir-fry the onion, garlic and mushrooms.

5) Stir in the light soy sauce, tamarind water, sugar, dark soy sauce and water or stock. Cook, stirring, for 4–5 minutes, until it thickens.

6) Crumble in the crispy noodles, mixing carefully. Pile on to a flat dish and scatter the egg strips, chilli and chives over the top.

Khanom Jin

Real khanom jin noodles are hard to find if you do not have a Thai supermarket nearby. The best substitute for them are Chinese thin rice noodles, which are round in section, not flat.

SERVES 4–6

200 g/7 oz	khanom jin noodles (see above)
1	small, green papaya, peeled and grated
a few	preserved vegetables (tang chi), chopped, optional
½	a cucumber, chopped
85 g/3 oz/1 cup	beansprouts
5	garlic cloves, sliced
3	shallots, thinly sliced
2 tablespoons	vegetable oil
2 tablespoons	Red Curry Paste (page 2)
2 tablespoons	soy sauce
2 tablespoons	tamarind purée
2 tablespoons	sugar
170 g/6 oz/2 cups	cut (into 5-cm/2 in lengths) yard-long or French beans (fine green beans)
140 g/5 oz/1 cup	finely chopped peanuts
250 ml/9 fl oz/1 cup	coconut milk (not cream)

1) Boil the noodles for 3–5 minutes, until just tender. Rinse briefly under running cold water. Drain well and pile on a serving dish.
2) Surround the noodles with the papaya, preserved vegetables, cucumber and beansprouts.
3) Fry the garlic and shallots in the oil until crisp. Remove and set aside.
4) Fry the Red Curry Paste for 1 minute.
5) Add the soy sauce, tamarind purée, sugar and beans. Cook, stirring, for 1 minute.
6) Add the peanuts and coconut milk and simmer for a few minutes. Add back the garlic and shallots and pour onto the noodles. Serve.

Egg-fried Noodles with Three Mushrooms

SERVES 4–6

60 ml/2 fl oz/¼ cup	vegetable oil
2	garlic cloves, thinly sliced
1	red onion, sliced
170 g/6 oz	egg noodles, blanched and drained
4	Kaffir lime leaves, shreddded
2 tablespoons	light soy sauce
100 g/3½ oz/1 cup	oyster mushrooms, trimmed
100 g/3½ oz/1 cup	shiitake mushrooms, trimmed
100 g/3½ oz/1 cup	chestnut (browncap) mushrooms, quartered
1 tablespoon	yellow bean sauce
2 teaspoons	lime juice
2 tablespoons	palm or light muscovado sugar
3	eggs
3	small fresh chillies, crushed and chopped

1) Pour half the oil into a wok. Fry the garlic and red onion until golden.
2) Add the noodles, lime leaves and soy sauce and stir-fry for 1 minute. Remove and keep warm.
3) Pour in the rest of the oil and fry the mushrooms very quickly.
4) Add the yellow bean sauce, lime juice and sugar.
5) When the sugar has dissolved, crack in the egg and mix gently.
6) Return the noodles to the pan and stir in the chillies. Serve straight away.

Sao Nam

This is a gloriously fruity sauce with noodles.

SERVES 4–6

3	garlic cloves, finely sliced
2	red onions, thinly sliced
2 tablespoons	vegetable oil
1 teaspoon	grated root ginger
200 g/7 oz/1 cup	fresh peeled pineapple cut into batons
3 tablespoons	light soy sauce
1 tablespoon	sugar
200 ml/7 fl oz/¾ cup	coconut milk
2 tablespoons	chopped fresh coriander (cilantro)
1	large fresh red chilli, slivered
115 g/4 oz	sen lek noodles (like tagliatelle), soaked and drained

1) Fry the garlic and onion in the oil.
2) Add the ginger and pineapple. Stir-fry for 2 minutes.
3) Add the soy sauce, sugar and coconut milk. Simmer for 2 minutes.
4) Stir in the coriander (cilantro), chilli and noodles. Turn about until combined and the noodles are just cooked. Serve.

Stir-fried Noodles with Aubergine (Eggplant)

The noodles in this dish are the wide, flat, ribbon-like ones.

SERVES 4–6

100 g/3½ oz	sen yai noodles
2	shallots, cut into rings
2	garlic cloves, crushed (minced)
2 tablespoons	vegetable oil
1–2 teaspoons	coarsely ground dried red chilli
1	medium aubergine (eggplant), cut into narrow strips
2 tablespoons	dark, rich – sweetened – soy sauce
50 g/2 oz/1 cup	Chinese leaves, shredded
1 tablespoon	chopped peanuts
1 tablespoon	chopped fresh coriander (cilantro)

1) Place the noodles in a large dish and pour boiling water over them. Leave to stand for 15 minutes (you can be preparing the vegetables during this time).
2) Fry the shallots and garlic in the oil until nutty brown.
3) Stir in the ground chilli. Add the aubergine (eggplant) and stir-fry for 2 minutes.
4) Add the soy sauce and Chinese leaves.
5) Drain and stir in the noodles. Cook until the noodles are tender, then serve with the peanuts and coriander (cilantro) sprinkled over the top.

Beancurd

Hot and Sour Beancurd

SERVES 4–6

1 teaspoon	grated root ginger
1 teaspoon	crushed (minced) garlic
1 teaspoon	thinly sliced lemongrass
2 tablespoons	vegetable oil
250 g/9 oz/1½ cups	cubed firm beancurd
85 g/3 oz/1 cup	chopped spring onions (scallions)
125 g/4 oz/1 cup	courgettes (zucchini) cut into strips
2	long fresh moderately hot red chillies, thinly sliced
100 g/3½ oz/½ cup	yellow bean sauce
50 g/2 oz/½ cup	tamarind purée
60 ml/2 fl oz/¼ cup	water
1 tablespoon	palm or muscovado sugar

1) Fry the ginger, garlic and lemongrass in the oil for 30 seconds.
2) Add the beancurd. Stir-fry until the edges begin to turn golden.
3) Add in the spring onions (scallions), courgettes (zucchini) and chillies. Stir-fry for a further 3 minutes.
4) Add the yellow bean sauce, tamarind purée, water and sugar. Cook, stirring, for another 2 minutes, then serve.

Beancurd in Blackbean Sauce

This is a much darker and more savoury version of braised bean-curd. It is particularly good with rice sticks – the wide, flat rice noodles. You can add an extra crunch by scattering a tablespoon of chopped cashews or peanuts over the top just before serving if you like.

SERVES 4–6

2 tablespoons	vegetable oil
250 g/9 oz/1½ cups	cubed firm beancurd
3	medium onions, chopped
3	garlic cloves, chopped
1 teaspoon	grated root ginger
1	fresh chilli, crushed and finely chopped
1 teaspoon	shredded lemongrass
3	medium carrots, sliced
125 g/4 oz/1 cup	mangetout (snow peas)
140 g/5 oz/¾ cup	blackbean sauce
90 ml/3 fl oz/¹/₃ cup	water

1) Heat the oil. Pat the beancurd dry and fry in batches in the oil until nicely browned. Drain.
2) Fry the onions, garlic, ginger, chilli and lemongrass for 1 minute.
3) Stir in the carrots and cook for 1 minute
4) Add the mangetout (snow peas) and cook for a further minute.
5) Add back the fried beancurd. Stir in the blackbean sauce and water. Allow to simmer briefly, then serve.

Beancurd Parcels I

Be careful not to confuse beancurd sheets with spring roll or won ton wrappers as they are not the same! Beancurd sheets need to be softened in warm water for about five minutes. They can be doing that while you prepare the filling.

SERVES 4

1 packet	beancurd sheets (see above)
50 g/2 oz/¾ cup	shredded shiitake mushrooms
50 g/2 oz/²/₃ cup	beansprouts
2	garlic cloves, chopped
30 g/1 oz/¼ cup	chopped spring onions
1 tablespoon	dark, rich – sweetened – soy sauce

1) Carefully separate the softened beancurd sheets and lay them out on baking parchment.
2) Mix together all the remaining ingredients and divide into 4 piles.
3) Place a pile of filling in the bottom left-hand corner of each beancurd sheet.
4) Roll the sheet up towards the top right-hand corner, folding the sides in to enclose the filling as you go and use the baking paper to help you lift the delicate sheets, gently peeling it off as you roll. Repeat with the other 3 sheets, then place the 4 parcels on a plate in a steamer over boiling water and steam for 15–20 minutes. Serve.

Beancurd Parcels II

As in Beancurd Parcels I (page 78), the beancurd sheets must be soaked before use to make them pliable.

SERVES 4

1 packet	beancurd sheets (page 78)
2	garlic cloves, crushed (minced)
½ teaspoon	grated root ginger
1	small fresh chilli, crushed and chopped
1 tablespoon	vegetable oil, plus extra for deep-frying
4	chestnut (browncap) mushrooms, thinly sliced
85 g/3 oz/½ cup	coarsely grated carrot
55 g/2 oz/1 cup	shredded Chinese leaves
1 tablespoon	dark soy sauce

GLUE

white of 1 egg or 1 teaspoon cornflour
(cornstarch) mixed with 1 tablespoon water

1) Carefully separate the beancurd sheets and lay them out on baking parchment.
2) Fry the garlic, ginger and chilli in the oil for 30 seconds.
3) Stir in the mushrooms, carrot and Chinese leaves in turn over a high heat.
4) Pour over the soy sauce and remove from the heat.
5) Divide the mixture into 4 equal portions. Place on the beancurd sheets and roll them up as described in the recipe for Beancurd Parcels I (page 78), but brush the last 5 cm/2 in of

the beancurd sheet with the egg white or cornflour (cornstarch) and water mixture to 'glue' it closed. Gently pat the parcels dry with kitchen paper and deep-fry in hot oil until golden and crisp.

Turmeric Beancurd

Fresh turmeric is sometimes found in larger supermarkets, looking a bit like orange root ginger. However, it is mainly sold dried and ground. If you are lucky enough to find fresh turmeric, be careful when you are preparing it – it will stain your hands.

SERVES 4–6

475 g/1 lb 1 oz/2½ cups	firm beancurd, cut into 1-cm/½-in thick slices
2 tablespoons	vegetable oil
4	garlic cloves, thinly sliced
1	large red onion, halved and thinly sliced
1	small fresh chilli, chopped
4 teaspoons	ground turmeric *or* 1 tablespoon freshly grated turmeric root
1 tablespoon	finely shredded lemongrass
2 tablespoons	light soy sauce
400-ml/14-oz can	coconut milk
2 tablespoons	roasted cashews
2 tablespoons	chopped fresh coriander (cilantro)

1) Fry the beancurd slices in the oil until golden. Drain.
2) Fry the garlic, onion and chilli for 1 minute.
3) Stir in the turmeric, lemongrass, soy sauce and beancurd.
4) Open the can of coconut milk without shaking it and spoon out 2 tablespoons of the thick coconut cream on the top and reserve.
5) Add the rest of the coconut milk to the pan. Stir. Simmer for 5 minutes, stirring from time to time. If necessary, add a little

water to prevent from sticking. Serve, topped with the reserved coconut cream, the cashews and coriander (cilantro).

Stuffed Chillies

I have never seen the big, pale hot Thai peppers required for this dish outside Thailand. However, I have come up with a couple of alternatives. If you don't like things too hot, you can make this dish with sweet (bell) peppers instead.

SERVES 4–6

4	Hungarian wax peppers or 6 large Kenya chillies
170 g/6 oz/1 cup	firm beancurd
2	garlic cloves, crushed (minced)
1 tablespoon	Red Curry Paste (page 2)
½ teaspoon	ground coriander
1	egg yolk
1 teaspoon	sugar
1 tablespoon	dark soy sauce
4 tablespoons	oil
2 tablespoons	finely shredded lemongrass

1) Cut the peppers or chillies in half lengthwise and remove the seeds.
2) Mash the beancurd with a fork and then work in the garlic, Red Curry Paste, ground coriander, egg yolk, sugar and soy sauce.
3) Pile into the peppers or chillies and either steam them for 20 minutes or bake them in a casserole dish (with 25 mm/¼ in of water poured around them, then tightly cover the dish) for 20 minutes at 400°F/200°C/gas 6.

4) Meanwhile, heat the oil in a small pan. Throw in the lemon-grass and fry until crisp. Drain immediately. The best way to do this is to tip the contents of the pan into a sieve (strainer) set over a heatproof bowl. Use it to garnish the cooked peppers or chillies.

Satay

For satay, it doesn't so much matter what you put on the skewers – mushrooms, beancurd and aubergine (eggplant) are all good – as the sauce you have with it. Scrupulous cooks will insist that you cannot make the sauce with peanut butter, but, as long as you use a good, wholefood, crunchy one, really, there isn't that much difference.

If time is not of the essence, you can marinate the filled skewers in a mixture of chillies, garlic, ginger and soy sauce.

SERVES 4–6

125 g/4 oz/1 cup	cubed aubergine (eggplant)
125 g/4 oz/1 cup	button mushrooms
285 g/10 oz/1½ cups	cubed firm beancurd
2 tablespoons	chilli-flavoured oil

FOR THE SAUCE

400-ml/14-oz can	coconut milk
2 tablespoons	Red Curry Paste (page 2)
1–2 tablespoons	palm or brown sugar
1 tablespoon	lime juice
2 tablespoons	peanut butter or 3–4 tablespoons roasted peanuts whizzed in a food processor
	salt or soy sauce, to taste

1) Thread the aubergine (eggplant), mushrooms and beancurd onto skewers. Brush liberally with the chilli-flavoured oil and grill (broil) or barbecue until browned.

2) Meanwhile, make the sauce. Open the can of coconut milk without shaking it and scoop 2 tablespoons of coconut cream off the top. Put it in a hot wok. Cook for 2 minutes, stirring.
3) Add the Red Curry Paste. Cook for 2 minutes, stirring.
4) Add the rest of the coconut milk, sugar, lime juice and peanut butter or peanuts. Stir and bring to the boil. Check the seasoning and serve with the skewered beancurd and vegetables.

Eggs

Chargrilled Eggs

This is a very simple idea for your next barbecue. Serve the eggs with Nam Prik or Red Chilli Sauce (pages 8, 10 and 11) and a salad. I note that in some districts Skewered Eggs are favoured, but this is easier!

1–2   eggs per person
salt or a chilli dipping sauce (see above)

1) When the charcoal is glowing hot and no longer flaming, place a rack approximately 5 cm/2 in above the coals. Prick the egg shells and place the eggs carefully on the rack. Turn from time to time. Remove after 15 minutes – 10 if you prefer them less well done.

2) When cool enough to handle, tap the shells gently and peel.

Stuffed Omelette I

The best stuffed omelette I ate was in the night market at Hua Hin. The stallholder had all her filling ingredients set out ready and two woks on the go the whole time. When the omelette was ready, she flipped it out onto a banana leaf, folded it over and handed it to you with a little plastic bag of chillies and cucumber in vinegar – the best fast food to go I have tasted! This recipe captures her delicious combination of flavours and textures.

SERVES 4

4 tablespoons	desiccated (shredded) coconut
1 tablespoon	sugar
1 tablespoon	vegetable oil
8	eggs
250 ml/9 fl oz/1 cup	soya or coconut milk
170 g/6 oz/2 cups	rinsed and drained beansprouts
4 tablespoons	finely diced pickled radish
70 g/2½ oz/½ cup	chopped roasted peanuts
4 tablespoons	chopped or shredded greens
pinch	of salt
pinch	of sugar
pinch	of chilli powder

1) Dry-roast the coconut and sugar until nicely browned. Scrape into a dish and wipe the wok clean.
2) Pour in the oil and heat the wok well, running the oil around the sides. Pour off any excess oil.

3) Beat 2 of the eggs well. Beat in a quarter of the soya or coconut milk.

4) Swirl the egg mixture into the hot wok, twisting and shaking it to cover the base and sides evenly. Cover for a minute.

5) Put a handful of beansprouts on the omelette, scatter on 1 tablespoon of the pickled radish, a quarter of the peanuts, 1 tablespoon of the dry-roasted coconut, 1 tablespoon of greens and a sprinkling of salt, sugar and chilli over the omelette.

6) Loosen the edges and dribble a *little* oil behind the omelette. Cover and cook for 1 minute before turning out. Eat immediately. Repeat 3 times more.

Stuffed Omelette II

This is a restaurant version of Stuffed Omelette I (page 89).

SERVES 2–4

1	red onion, quartered
125 g/4 oz/1 cup	chestnut mushrooms
2	garlic cloves
1 teaspoon	soy sauce
½ teaspoon	ground white pepper
1 teaspoon	palm or light muscovado sugar
3 tablespoons	vegetable oil
1	tomato, chopped
3	eggs, beaten

1) Put the onion, mushrooms, garlic, soy sauce, pepper, sugar and 2 tablespoons of the oil into a blender or food processor and process until finely chopped together.

2) Scrape into a preheated wok and stir-fry for 1 minute.

3) Add the tomato and simmer gently while cooking the eggs.

4) Heat the remaining oil in a large frying pan or clean wok. Pour in the egg and run it around to cover the base of the pan. When set, spoon the onion and mushroom mixture into the middle of the omelette. Neatly fold in the sides to make a square envelope. Turn it out onto a plate and serve.

Deep-fried Eggs

A side-order of eggs with vegetable, noodle, rice or curry dishes is not uncommon in Thai eating houses. Sometimes it is a simple egg fried in the wok or sometimes these golden Deep-fried Eggs arrive. If you want to make a meal of the eggs, though, serve one and a half or two per person and accompany them with some green salad or one of the yams (mixed salads) given in Chapter 3 and a hot and spicy dipping sauce.

Bottled quails' eggs can also be used. Simply drain them, pat them dry and fry in the same way as given in the recipe. Serve them on cocktail sticks with a fiery dipping sauce for a wonderful appetizer.

6–8 eggs
vegetable oil, for deep-frying

1) Place the eggs in boiling water and cook for 5–6 minutes. Place immediately into a bowl of cold water.
2) Heat sufficient oil to cover the eggs well in a wok or deep-fat fryer.
3) Meanwhile, peel the eggs. Gently dry on some kitchen paper, then fry until crisp and golden on the outside. Drain, halve and serve immediately.

Egg Custard

This is a comforting dish and a mild one – no chillies. Serve it as a contrast to a Mussaman or green curry.

SERVES 4–6

170 g/6 oz/1 cup	ready-made Italian gnocchi
1	large red onion, chopped
1 tablespoon	oil
4	eggs, beaten with 60 ml/2 fl oz/¼ cup water
1 tablespoon	chopped fresh coriander (cilantro)
2 tablespoons	mushroom ketchup or light soy sauce

1) Bring a large pan of water to the boil. Drop in the gnocchi and cook for 5 minutes.
2) Meanwhile, fry the onion quickly in the oil.
3) Take the gnocchi out with a slotted spoon and stand a steamer over the boiling water.
4) Gently combine the eggs and water with the onion, gnocchi, coriander (cilantro) and mushroom ketchup or soy sauce. Pour the mixture into a heatproof bowl and stand in the steamer until the eggs are set – approximately 15–18 minutes.

Cooks' Note
If you are particularly pressed for time, you can add the onions raw.

Polished Eggs

Startlingly dark and glistening eggs, like polished mahogany. Very tasty on their own or in Wun Sen Khai Yam (page 95).

SERVES 4–6

4	large (extra large) (even duck eggs) or 8 small (bantam) hard-boiled (hard-cooked) eggs, peeled
4	garlic cloves, crushed (minced)
2 tablespoons	vegetable oil
2 tablespoons	palm or dark muscovado sugar
4 tablespoons	dark, rich – sweetened – soy sauce

1) Score tight spirals into the whites of the eggs, from the tops to the bottoms, using a sharp knife.
2) Fry the garlic in the oil until it just starts to change colour.
3) Add the sugar and soy sauce and stir well.
4) Add the eggs and turn them about in the sauce so that they are evenly covered. When they are nice and dark and the sauce is thick and syrupy, take them out and serve.

Wun Sen Khai Yam

Wun sen are the wiry, very thin, thread-like noodles.

SERVES 4

100 g/3½ oz	wun sen noodles, soaked and drained
85 g/3 oz/1 cup	blanched beansprouts
4	spring onions (scallions), shredded
2	garlic cloves, crushed (minced)
	juice of 1 lime
2 tablespoons	light soy sauce
4	Polished Eggs (page 94)
1	fresh red chilli, slivered

1) Drop the noodles into boiling water, count to 3, then drain. Rinse them briefly under running cold water and drain well.
2) Mix with the beansprouts, spring onions (scallions), garlic, lime juice and soy sauce.
3) Form into a nest on a serving plate. Place the eggs in the centre and scatter the chilli slivers over the top.

Stir-fried Eggs and Mouse Ears

Don't panic, mouse ears are Chinese black fungus! They are sold dried, black on one side, velvety grey on the other, just like a mouse's ear.

Soaking the mushrooms is what takes the most time in this recipe – everything else is cooked in a flash. Put the mushrooms to soak, cook a rice or noodle dish and then do the eggs at the last minute.

SERVES 4–6

1 tablespoon	dried black fungus, or mouse ears
125 ml/4½ fl oz/½ cup	boiling water
4	garlic cloves, sliced
1	shallot, finely sliced
2 tablespoons	vegetable oil
2 tablespoons	dark soy sauce
85 g/3 oz/1 cup	beansprouts
3	eggs, lightly beaten

1) Soak the fungus in the boiling water for 20 minutes.
2) Drain, saving the liquor for stock (freeze if not using it straight away). Shred it.
3) Fry the garlic and shallot in the oil.
4) Add the soy sauce, fungus strips and beansprouts. Stir-fry for 1 minute.
5) Add the eggs. Continue to stir-fry until the eggs are done. Serve with Chilli Pickle (page 14).

Quails' Eggs and Straw Mushrooms

This may sound like one of the more exotic recipes in this book, but it is made very quickly and simply.

SERVES 4–6

2	shallots, chopped
2 tablespoons	vegetable oil
1 tablespoon	Red Curry Paste (page 2)
200-g/7-oz can	straw mushrooms
200 ml/7 fl oz/¾ cup	coconut milk
60 ml/2 fl oz/¼ cup	tomato ketchup
60 ml/2 fl oz/¼ cup	water
1 tablespoon	light soy sauce or 1 teaspoon salt
1 tablespoon	palm sugar
400-g/14-oz jar	quails' eggs, drained
small bunch	of fresh coriander (cilantro)

1) Fry the shallots in the oil until softened and colouring.
2) Add the Red Curry Paste. Stir-fry for 30 seconds.
3) Add, in turn and while stirring, the straw mushrooms, coconut milk, ketchup, water, soy sauce or salt and sugar. Simmer.
4) Prick the eggs all over with a needle and drop into the sauce. Cook gently for 4 minutes. Serve garnished with the coriander (cilantro).

Thai Toast

As a rule, Thais don't seem to eat much bread – the exceptions being when they visit the American-style diners in the cities. However, these crisp and tasty toasts – usually made with pork or prawn – are very popular.

SERVES 4–6

115 g/4 oz/1 cup	roughly broken up mushrooms
1	onion, quartered
1–2	eggs (see step 3 of method below)
½ teaspoon	ground black pepper
½ teaspoon	ground coriander
1 teaspoon	salt
3 slices	white bread, quartered
approximately 3 tablespoons	white sesame seeds
	vegetable oil, for deep-frying

1) Mince the mushrooms and onion in a blender or food processor in short bursts.
2) Add 1 egg, the pepper, coriander and salt. Process to mix well together.
3) Spread on the bread and pat on a teaspoon of sesame seeds. If liked, dip in the remaining egg (beaten). Deep-fry until crisp. Drain and serve.

Frittered and Fried

Crisp Aubergine (Eggplant)

SERVES 4–6

4	small fresh red chillies, deseeded
6	garlic cloves
2 tablespoons	coconut cream (page 5)
2 tablespoons	palm sugar
2 tablespoons	mushroom ketchup or light soy sauce if unavailable
2 tablespoons	tamarind purée
1	large, long aubergine (eggplant), cut lengthwise into 1-cm/½-in thick slices
1 tablespoon	rice flour
	oil, for deep-frying

1) Chop up the chillies and garlic in a blender or food processor to form a very rough paste.

2) Put the coconut cream into a hot wok. Stir and cook until it begins to separate.

3) Add the chilli and garlic mixture. Cook for 1 minute.

4) Stir in the sugar and cook until it has melted.

5) Stir in the mushroom ketchup or soy sauce and the tamarind purée. Keep just warm.

6) Heat sufficient oil in which to deep-fry the aubergine (eggplant) slices.

7) Meanwhile, dust the aubergine (eggplant) slices with the rice flour and, when the oil is hot enough, deep-fry quickly until crisp and golden. Drain on kitchen paper, lay on a plate and top with the sauce.

Corncakes

Thais use sweetcorn in both sweet and savoury dishes. You will find the kernels in coconut custards and here in these spicy fritters.

SERVES 4–6

395 g/14 oz/2 cups	well-drained canned sweetcorn
2 tablespoons	rice flour
1	egg
1	garlic clove, crushed (minced)
1 teaspoon	ground dried red chillies
4	Kaffir lime leaves, finely shredded
	oil, for deep-frying

1) Combine the sweetcorn, rice flour, egg, garlic and ground chillies in a blender or food processor. Whizz to a coarse paste. Stir in the lime leaves.
2) Drop teaspoonfuls of the mixture into hot oil. Drain and serve.

Courgette (Zucchini) Fritters

This recipe is just right for home gardeners whose courgettes (zucchini) will insist on marrowdom as it is best made using those 5 cm (2 in) in diameter. You can also cook aubergines (eggplants) in the same way.

Serve these with either Nam Prik or Red Chilli Sauce (pages 8, 10 and 11).

SERVES 4–6

1–2 large courgettes (zucchini) – see above

1 large (extra large) egg, beaten

oil, for deep-frying

1) Slice the courgettes (zucchini) thickly on the diagonal so you have oval slices 5 mm/$^1/_4$ in thick.

2) Heat oil to 185°C/365°F.

3) Dip the courgette (zucchini) slices in the beaten egg. Fry, in batches, until crisp and golden.

Fried Wontons

This recipe can only make it into this book of quick dishes because wonton squares are available from Chinese grocers (they are about 7.5 cm (3 in) square). The filling is made, very fast, in a blender or food processor.

Serve these delicious Fried Wontons with Nam Prik or Red Chilli Sauce (pages 8, 10 and 11).

SERVES 4–6

170 g/6 oz/1½ cups	mushrooms broken up roughly
1	red onion, quartered
2	garlic cloves, crushed (minced)
1	egg, separated
1 teaspoon	light soy sauce
½ teaspoon	ground coriander
	oil, for deep-frying
1 packet	of about 20 wonton squares

1) Put the mushrooms, onion, garlic, egg yolk, soy sauce and coriander into a blender or food processor and process, in bursts, to make a coarse paste.

2) Heat oil steadily to 185°C/365°F.

3) Meanwhile, place a teaspoon of the paste in the centre of each wonton square. Beat the egg white lightly and brush it around the edges. Fold to form a triangle, pinching to seal. Fry a few at a time for about 5 minutes, until crisp and golden.

Fried Crispy

Fried Crispy, *The Lonely Planet Guide to Thailand* tells me, is the translation of krabawng jaw – a speciality of Mae Sot in North-West Thailand, virtually on the border with Myanmar (Burma).

SERVES 4–6

2 tablespoons	tamarind purée
2 tablespoons	dark soy sauce
2 tablespoons	palm or brown sugar
2 tablespoons	chopped roasted peanuts
1–2 teaspoons	coarsely ground dried red chillies
1	lime
1	egg
3 tablespoons	rice flour
3 tablespoons	cornflour (cornstarch)
	water, as required
	vegetable oil, for deep-frying
500 g/1 lb 2 oz/4 cups	peeled, deseeded squash, pumpkin or papaya cut into large cubes

1) Warm the tamarind purée, soy sauce and sugar together until the sugar has melted and all the ingredients have mixed together.

2) Stir in the peanuts and ground chillies.

3) Quarter the lime and add a squeeze of juice to the sauce, to taste.

4) Make a thick batter with the egg, flours and a little water.

5) Heat oil.

6) Meanwhile, dip the cubes in the batter and, when the oil is hot enough, cook until 'fried crispy'. Drain and serve hot with the dipping sauce and the rest of the lime.

Spring Rolls

Spring Rolls spread to Thailand via neighbouring Vietnam and are now part of the national diet. Spring roll wrappers can be found in the freezer cabinet at larger supermarkets and at oriental stores. If you are unable to find any, you can use filo pastry sheets instead and then bake or fry them.

SERVES 4–6

3	garlic cloves, crushed (minced)
2 tablespoons	vegetable oil, plus extra for deep-frying
255 g/9 oz/2 cups	leeks cut into 5-cm/2-in lengths and shredded
85 g/3 oz/1 cup	sliced mushrooms
170 g/6 oz/1 cup	coarsely grated carrots
2 tablespoons	light soy sauce
1 teaspoon	palm or brown sugar
1 teaspoon	ground coriander
55 g/2 oz	thin rice vermicelli – sen mee – soaked and drained
250-g/9-oz packet	spring roll wrappers, thawed
1	egg, beaten

1) Fry the garlic in the 2 tablespoons of oil.
2) When golden, stir-fry the leeks, mushrooms and carrots for 3 minutes.
3) Add the soy sauce, sugar, coriander and vermicelli. Cook for a couple of minutes.
4) Heat oil for deep frying.
5) Meanwhile, lay the spring roll wrappers in a tea towel (dish towel) to keep them from drying out.
6) Working with 1 at a time, put a mound of filling in one corner. Fold the spring roll wrapper over it and roll up on the diagonal, towards the opposite corner, tucking the sides in as you go. Seal by brushing the opposite corner with the beaten egg. If you cannot visualize this, think of how the assistant wraps bottles in the off licence (liquor store).
7) Deep-fry until crisp and golden. Alternatively, you can steam on a heatproof plate.

Vegetable Fritters

There are many different ways of serving these batter-coated vegetables – none nicer than as street food in the night market in a cone of paper with bottled sweet chilli sauce instead of tomato ketchup. There are certainly overtones of Japanese tempura here.

SERVES 4–6

500 g/1 lb 2 oz	mixed vegetables (broccoli, cauliflower, asparagus, mushrooms, celery, beans, whole chillies, even, if brave, etc.), divided into florets or cut into big, bite-sized pieces
3	garlic cloves, crushed (minced)
3	small fresh chillies, crushed and chopped
2 tablespoons	soy sauce
	vegetable oil, for deep-frying
1	egg
115 ml/4 fl oz/½ cup	water
100 g/3½ oz/2/3 cup	self-raising flour (self-rising flour)
30 g/1 oz/¼ cup	cornflour (cornstarch)
1 teaspoon	baking powder

1) Put the prepared vegetables onto a large plate.
2) Mix together the garlic, chillies and soy sauce. Drizzle over the vegetables, turning them about as if dressing a salad. Allow to stand.
3) Heat oil.
4) Mix together the egg and water.
5) Sift in the flours and baking powder. Mix quickly together with a fork. Don't beat – just mix together, as if making muffins.
6) Dip the vegetables in the batter, then fry in the hot oil until crisp and golden. Don't try to fry too many at once. Drop them in one at a time so that the temperature of the oil does not drop.

Stir-fries

Aubergine (Eggplant) and Basil Stir-fry

This is very much a side dish – there is not a huge amount and it is quite hot. You can always double the quantities if you really like it.

SERVES 4–6

2	large fresh hot red chillies
4	garlic cloves, peeled
2 tablespoons	vegetable oil
1	large aubergine (eggplant), cut into thin strips
2 tablespoons	light soy sauce
1 tablespoon	palm or light muscovado sugar
15 g/½ oz/½ cup	fresh basil leaves (the smaller leaved holy basil if available)

1) Pound or blend the chillies and garlic to make a rough paste.
2) Fry in the oil for 1 minute.
3) Add the aubergine (eggplant) strips and stir-fry for 3 minutes.
4) Add the soy sauce and sugar. Cook for another minute, then stir in the basil leaves and serve.

Yellow Bean and Sweet Potato Stir-fry

SERVES 4–6

2 tablespoons	groundnut oil
1 stem	lemongrass, peeled and chopped
1 teaspoon	grated root ginger
2	garlic cloves, sliced
1	medium Spanish or red onion, chopped
500 g/1 lb 2 oz/3¼ cups	peeled sweet potatoes cut into batons
2 tablespoons	sesame seeds
2 tablespoons	yellow bean sauce
2 tablespoons	water
a handful	of fresh coriander (cilantro), roughly torn
1	small fresh red chilli, finely chopped

1) Heat the oil in a wok. Stir in the lemongrass, ginger, garlic and onion. Fry for 1 minute.

2) Stir in the sweet potato. Fry briskly, while shaking or stirring, for a couple of minutes.

3) Add the sesame seeds. Fry for another couple of minutes.

4) Add the yellow bean sauce and water. Simmer until the sweet potato is just tender, adding a very little extra water if necessary to prevent it sticking.

5) Stir in the coriander (cilantro), scatter the finely chopped chilli over the top. Serve.

Vegetables Fried in Green Curry Paste

A great way to use up odd vegetables – pick any combination you like.

SERVES 4–6

2 tablespoons	Green Curry Paste (page 4)
2 tablespoons	vegetable oil
450 g/1 lb	mixed fresh vegetables (carrots, potatoes, cauliflower, broccoli, onions, beans, mangetout (snow peas), etc.), sliced
4 tablespoons	coconut milk
2 tablespoons	palm or brown sugar
3 tablespoons	light soy sauce
15 g/½ oz/½ cup	fresh basil leaves
1	medium fresh red chilli, slivered

1) Fry the Green Curry Paste in the oil for 1 minute.
2) Add the vegetables a few at a time, stirring.
3) Add the coconut milk, sugar and soy sauce. Stir-fry until the vegetables are just cooked, adding a little water if necessary to prevent them from sticking.
4) Add the basil and chilli and serve immediately.

Stir-fried Broccoli and Beansprouts

An ultra-quick dish. If you cook it for an even shorter time and add the juice of a lime, you can serve it as a salad – yam in Thai.

SERVES 4–6

2 tablespoons	vegetable oil
2	garlic cloves, peeled and sliced
1 teaspoon	coarsely ground dried red chilli
100 g/3½ oz/1 cup	broccoli stems, sliced
75 g/2¾ oz/1 cup	small broccoli florets
2 tablespoons	roasted cashew nuts
170 g/6 oz/2 cups	beansprouts, rinsed
1 tablespoon	soy sauce

1) Heat the oil, fry the garlic until just colouring.
2) Stir in the ground chilli, then add the broccoli stems. Stir-fry for 2 minutes.
3) Add the florets and stir-fry for 30 seconds.
4) Add the cashews, then the beansprouts and soy sauce. Cook for a minute more and serve still *al dente*.

Braised Leeks with Ginger and Cashews

SERVES 4–6

4	garlic cloves, crushed (minced)
2.5-cm/1-in piece	root ginger, finely sliced into matchsticks
2 tablespoons	vegetable oil
1	small fresh chilli, chopped
500 g/1 lb 2 oz/4 cups	cleaned and cut (into 5-cm/2-in lengths) baby leeks
2 tablespoons	light soy sauce
2 tablespoons	palm or brown sugar
2 tablespoons	lime juice
2 tablespoons	water
100 g/3½ oz/¾ cup	roasted cashews

1) Fry the garlic and ginger in the oil until just starting to colour.
2) Add the chilli and leeks. Stir-fry for 2 minutes.
3) Add the soy sauce, sugar, lime juice and water and simmer until the leeks are just tender.
4) Stir in the cashews and cook 30 seconds more. Serve.

Rich Mushroom and Basil Stir-fry

This is very similar to Aubergine (Eggplant) and Basil Stir-fry (page 112), but the result is darker and richer.

SERVES 4–6

	6 garlic cloves, peeled and roughly chopped
	2 small fresh hot red or green chillies, roughly chopped
2 tablespoons	vegetable oil
225 g/8 oz/2 cups	large dark flat mushrooms, sliced
2	large fresh moderately hot red chillies, sliced
2 tablespoons	light soy sauce
1 tablespoon	dark, rich – sweetened – soy sauce
30 g/1 oz/1 cup	fresh basil leaves

1) Pound the garlic and small chillies together. You can do this with a rolling pin and a wooden board if you do not have a mortar and pestle. Just break them up a bit – you do not need to make a paste.

2) Fry the garlic and small chillies in the oil for about 30 seconds.

3) Add the mushrooms. Stir-fry for 3 minutes.

4) Add the large sliced chillies. Cook for 1 minute.

5) Add the soy sauces. If the mushrooms are very dry, you might need to add a spoon or two of water.

6) Stir in the basil and serve.

Paad Paag See Sa Hai – Fried Vegetable Quintet

Using ready prepared baby vegetables from the supermarket will speed up the preparation of this dish. Stir-frying each vegetable separately is nicer, but, if you are pushed for time, just pop all of them into the wok at once.

Serve this dish with simple Plain Rice (page 54) or noodles.

SERVES 4–6

2 tablespoons	vegetable oil
1 bunch	of spring onions (scallions), trimmed
115 g/4 oz/1 cup	carrots cut into thin 5-cm/2-in long strips
225 g/8 oz/2 cups	broccoli florets
225 g/8 oz/1 cup	asparagus cut into 5-cm/2-in lengths
115 g/4 oz/1 cup	halved mushrooms (shiitake or browncap)
2 tablespoons	light soy sauce
2 tablespoons	mushroom ketchup
4 tablespoons	water
2 tablespoons	palm sugar or light muscovado if unavailable

1) Heat half the oil in the wok. Stir-fry the spring onions (scallions) until they just begin to colour. Remove them to a warmed serving platter. Keep warm.

2) Stir-fry the carrots for about 2 minutes, until just barely softened. Arrange on the platter next to the spring onions (scallions).

3) Cook the remaining vegetables in turn, adding a little more oil as necessary.

4) When all the vegetables have been cooked, add the remaining ingredients to the wok, stirring well to combine, and melt the sugar. Allow to bubble and become slightly syrupy. Pour over the vegetables and serve.

Fried Watercress

We tend to think of watercress only in terms of soup and salad, but its peppery leaves are a bonus as a green vegetable. Here it is perked up further with the addition of ginger.

If you grow nasturtiums with their showy orange and yellow flowers, remember, when cutting its rambling back, that you can cook and eat the trimmings using this recipe. Use a flower to decorate the plate – it is edible, too.

SERVES 4–6

2	garlic cloves, crushed (minced)
1 teaspoon	grated root ginger
2 tablespoons	vegetable oil
3 bunches	of watercress, trimmed, washed and patted dry
1 teaspoon	coarsely ground dried red chilli
good pinch	of salt

1) Fry the garlic and ginger in the oil until changing colour.
2) Add the watercress and stir-fry for 1 minute.
3) Sprinkle the chilli and salt over the top. Serve immediately.

Stir-fried Cabbage

SERVES 4–6

4	garlic cloves, sliced
2 tablespoons	vegetable oil
140 g/5 oz/¾ cup	sliced firm beancurd cut into strips
2 tablespoons	dark soy sauce
1 tablespoon	palm or light muscovado sugar
¼ teaspoon	freshly ground black pepper
225 g/8 oz/4 cups	shredded and blanched cabbage

1) Fry the garlic in the oil until browning.
2) Stir-fry the beancurd.
3) Add the soy sauce, sugar and pepper.
4) Stir-fry the cabbage until just tender. Serve.

Nor Mai Pad – Fried Asparagus

Asparagus is treated with a certain amount of reverence in many Western kitchens, where it is only steamed or boiled. In Hong Kong, it is fried with sesame oil and in Thailand you might find it holding its own with garlic and chillies. Try it, it is an eye-opening experience.

SERVES 4–6

2	garlic cloves, peeled and halved lengthwise
2	small fresh chillies, halved and deseeded
2 tablespoons	vegetable oil
500 g/1 lb 2 oz	fresh asparagus (fine spears, even as thin as sprue, work best), trimmed

1) Crush the garlic and chillies with the flat of a knife, then chop.
2) Fry in the hot oil for 30 seconds.
3) Add the asparagus. Stir-fry for about 4 minutes (less if using sprue), until just tender. If there is a serious tendency to sticking, add 1 tablespoon of water – no more.

Morning Glory in Garlic, Chilli and Yellow Bean Sauce

You might find morning glory at an ethnic grocer's under the name of water spinach. It has pointy leaves and lovely crunchy stems. If you can't get it, use Ruby or Swiss chard.

SERVES 4–6

3	garlic cloves, sliced
2	small fresh chillies, sliced
2 tablespoons	vegetable oil
2 tablespoons	light soy sauce
2 tablespoons	yellow bean sauce
1 tablespoon	sugar
340 g/12 oz/6 cups	blanched and cut (into 7.5-cm/3-in lengths) morning glory (water spinach)

1) Fry the garlic and chillies in the oil.
2) Add the soy sauce, yellow bean sauce and sugar. Stir around.
3) Add and stir-fry the morning glory for 2–3 minutes. Serve.

Yard-long Beans in Chilli and Coconut

Yard-long beans are very long green beans. If you cannot get them, use Kenya, Helda or runner beans (green beans). Yellow wax beans are also extremely good prepared this way.

SERVES 4–6

2 tablespoons	coconut cream
1 tablespoon	Red Curry Paste (page 2)
500 g/1 lb 2 oz/4 cups	cut (into 2.5-cm/1-in lengths) yard-long beans
1 teaspoon	sugar
1 tablespoon	light soy sauce

1) Heat the coconut cream in a wok, stirring, over a high heat for 1 minute.
2) Add the Red Curry Paste and cook for 2 minutes.
3) Stir in the beans, sugar and soy sauce. Cook, stirring, until the beans are just tender. Add a small amount of water to prevent sticking if necessary.

Vegetable Stir-fry with
Tamarind and Peanut Sauce

This is a very Malay-influenced dish.

SERVES 4–6

2	garlic cloves, shredded
4 slices	root ginger, shredded
2	small fresh chillies, finely chopped
2 tablespoons	vegetable oil
4	small red onions, trimmed and quartered
250 g/9 oz/2 cups	cut (into 5-cm/2-in lengths) yard-long beans
125 g/4 oz/1 cup	sugar-snap peas
170 g/6 oz/3 cups	broccoli florets
100 g/3½ oz/½ cup	chopped pineapple – canned unsweetened if fresh not available
1 tablespoon	soy sauce
1 tablespoon	palm or soft brown sugar
85 g/3 oz/¾ cup	ground roasted peanuts *or* 2 tablespoons wholefood crunchy peanut butter
2 tablespoons	tamarind purée
about 125 ml/4 fl oz/½ cup	water

1) Fry the garlic, ginger and chillies in the oil until browning.
2) Stir-fry the rest of the vegetables, adding each in turn and finish with the pineapple. Stir in the soy sauce, sugar, peanuts or peanut butter, tamarind purée and enough water to sauce the vegetables. Simmer, then serve.

Het Fang Ping

Ideally this recipe should be made with fresh straw mushrooms. However, you will probably only be able to find these in cans. If you do use the canned ones, use half canned and half fresh closed chestnut (browncap) or ordinary button mushrooms.

Straw mushrooms are so called because they are grown on the rice 'straw'. The Chinese name is very aptly descriptive, meaning one mushroom on top of another. Cut a straw mushroom in half and you will immediately see the reason for this name.

SERVES 4 AS AN APPETIZER

16	straw mushrooms or see above – if the canned ones are very small, double the quantity
4	old lemongrass stems or 4 bamboo skewers
3 tablespoons	oil
6	garlic cloves, crushed (minced)
2	large fresh red chillies, roughly chopped
2 tablespoons	palm or brown sugar
2 tablespoons	light soy sauce
2 tablespoons	tamarind purée

1) Push 4 mushrooms onto each lemongrass stem or skewer. Brush them with 1 tablespoon of the oil. Place under a grill (broiler) or over charcoal, turning until nicely roasted.
2) Meanwhile, fry the garlic and chillies in the remaining oil until browned.
3) Pour into a blender or food processor and whizz with the rest of the ingredients. Serve with the mushrooms.

Desserts, Drinks and Nibbles

Coconut Custard with Fried Shallots

Yes, fried shallots! Try it before you decide you don't like it.

SERVES 6

400-ml/14-oz can	coconut milk
4 tablespoons	sugar, plus extra as required
4	eggs, beaten
2	shallots, finely sliced
1 teaspoon	oil

1) Preheat the oven to 200°C/400°F/Gas 6.
2) Heat the coconut milk and sugar until just about to boil.
3) Whisk onto the eggs and pour into 6 small ramekins.
4) Stand the ramekins in a roasting tin of boiling water. Bake in the preheated oven for 15–20 minutes, until set.
5) Meanwhile, fry the shallots in the oil, very slowly, until a deep brown. Stir from time to time to avoid sticking. Add a little sugar, if necessary, at the end of cooking.
6) Serve the custards with a teaspoon of shallots on top in the centre.

Fried Bananas

Fried bananas are a snack food found in street markets and a well-loved pudding.

Ideally, you should use slightly underripe fig bananas – the stubby sweet ones – for this dish, but larger ones will do, just cut them in half before slicing lengthwise. If you are lucky enough to find 'princess' fingernail' bananas, dip them and fry them whole.

SERVES 8

	oil, for deep-frying
3 tablespoons	rice flour
3 tablespoons	cornflour (cornstarch)
1	egg, beaten
60 ml/2 fl oz/¼ cup	water
8	small or 4 ordinary bananas (see above)
1	lime, cut into wedges
	sugar, to serve

1) Heat oil.
2) Meanwhile, mix together the flours, egg and water to form a smooth batter.
3) Slice the bananas, lengthwise, into about 5-mm/¼-in thick slices.
4) Dip in the batter and drop into the hot oil. Fry until golden. Serve with the lime and sugar.

Durian

Durian would certainly be a talking point at your dinner table. For a start, it probably would not fit into your fruit bowl. The prehistoric-looking monster can weigh in at 4.5 kg (10 lbs)! The stegosaurus of the fruit world looks inedible in its leathery brown skin covered in chunky spikes and when it is ripe, it *smells* inedible, too! Avoid any that have split – you'll have no difficulty finding which these are as your nose will tell you, very emphatically. Be careful to avoid getting the juice on your clothes – it leaves an indelible stain.

This said, if you are brave enough to try this extraordinary fruit, you may discover why some people become quite passionate about it.

SERVES 4–6

1 ripe, but not overripe, durian (see above)

1) Using a large, sharp knife, quarter the durian. Spoon out the flesh and seeds (the seeds can be roasted, if desired, and served as an appetizer).
2) Serve the rich, creamy flesh on its own or as part of a fruit plate.

Coconut Rice and Mango

A lovely, creamy rice pudding, with the juicy, fragrant mango slices providing a wonderful, tropical contrast. Alternatively, you can serve the rice with pineapple slices. If you like, grill (broil) the pineapple with a little palm or brown sugar sprinkled on it first.

True Thai glutinous or sticky rice requires presoaking and steaming, so this is a speedier version but it is still quite similar to the original.

SERVES 4–6

55 g/2 oz/¼ cup	pudding (short-grain) rice
55 g/2 oz/¼ cup	creamed coconut (the solid 'soap bar' lookalike)
55 g/2 oz/¼ cup	sugar
400 ml/14 fl oz/1¾ cups	water
1 teaspoon	rosewater, if liked
2	ripe mangoes, peeled and sliced, or canned if fresh unavailable

1) Put the rice, coconut, sugar and water into a pan.
2) Over a medium heat, stirring occasionally, cook until the coconut and sugar have melted.
3) Simmer and stir from time to time. Cook for 25 minutes.
4) Stir in the rosewater. Serve immediately with the mango slices. Alternatively, this rice can be served cold.

Coconut Milk and Bananas

You can find this simple pudding in the chilled counter of most cheap restaurants in Thailand. You can eat it hot, warm or well chilled. It is not so far removed from the Western nursery favourite, bananas and custard.

SERVES 4–6

340 ml/12 fl oz/1½ cups	water
4 tablespoons	caster (granulated) sugar
400-ml/14-oz can	coconut milk
1 teaspoon	rosewater or strip of lime peel, if liked
6	fig bananas or 3 ripe ordinary ones, cut into 5-cm/2-in lengths

1) Mix the water and sugar together in a pan. Stir until dissolved, then bring to the boil.
2) Stir in the coconut milk and rosewater or lime peel, if using. Simmer for 2 minutes.
3) Add the bananas and cook gently for a further 3 minutes.

Coconut Oysters

Many street vendors have what look to be enormous cast iron escargot pans heating over braziers. Into each depression they pour coconut batter. The outside forms a crisp shell while the middle is custardy-soft. The following recipe is based on this street food, but has been adapted for speed and to make it suitable for cooking at home.

Serve three to a plate with some fried coconut and mango slices.

SERVES 4–6

	oil, for greasing
570 ml/1 pint/2½ cups	coconut milk
3	eggs
100 g/3½ oz/⅔ cup	rice flour
115 g/4 oz/½ cup	caster (granulated) sugar

1) Preheat the oven to 220°C/425°F/Gas 7.
2) At the same time, pour a little oil into each cup of a 12-hole cast iron or other heavy muffin or popover pan and place it in the oven to heat.
3) Beat all the other ingredients together very well or whizz in a blender.
4) Fill each of the hot muffin cups half-way. Bake in the preheated oven for 15 minutes. Loosen carefully around the edges with a round-bladed knife and tip them out.

Coconut Crêpes

On the street in Thailand, you can find vendors selling these little pancakes in delicate hues of pink and green. Fillings might consist of goopy coconut custard or fried desiccated (shredded) coconut with sugar or sweetcorn and nuts. I prefer them with a little lime or fresh mango purée.

SERVES 4–6

55 g/2 oz/¹/₃ cup	rice flour
1	egg
200 ml/7 fl oz/¾ cup	coconut milk
2 tablespoons	caster (granulated) sugar
	oil, for greasing

1) Whizz the rice flour, egg, coconut milk and sugar in a blender for 60 seconds, until well blended and smooth. Otherwise, beat well by hand to make a smooth batter. Leave to stand for 10 minutes.
2) Heat a heavy, oiled frying pan over a moderate heat. When hot, pour in a tablespoon of the batter. Fry until speckledy golden, then flip over and fry the other side. Repeat, using up the rest of the batter. Using 2 pans will speed the process up.

Fruit Plate

Dessert doesn't come simpler than this, and your guests peel the fruit themselves, so preparation is minimal, too! Simply give each diner a plate and a small sharp knife. Provide napkins and fingerbowls.

Although the fruits used look very different on the outside – carved, wooden-looking mangosteen, figured velvet lychees and curly-headed rambutans – the insides are more similar.

SERVES 4–6

8 mangosteen

8 fresh lychees

8 rambutans

fresh mint or lemon balm leaves, to decorate

1) Arrange the fruit in a pile on a lovely plate.
2) Tuck in the leaves to decorate.

Papaya Plate

Serve this delightfully simple dish as a dessert, for breakfast or as a salad. When buying the papayas for it, the skin of ripe ones will have turned yellow and they will be softish and fragrant.

SERVES 4–6

2 large, ripe papayas (see above)
1 lime
  caster (granulated) sugar, to taste

1) Quarter the papayas lengthwise and scrape out the seeds. Peel off the skin and cut the flesh into thin slices. Arrange in overlapping rows on a large platter.

2) Using a zester, remove the zest from the lime and scatter over the papaya slices, then squeeze the juice over them. Sprinkle with a little sugar and leave for 10 minutes. Serve at room temperature or chilled.

Sweet Bananas

You need a sweet tooth to appreciate this dish. If you find it too cloying, try adding three whole cardamom pods to the syrup or some lime zest – this is not wholly authentic, but I prefer it.

SERVES 4–6

200 g/7 oz/1 cup	sugar
340 ml/12 fl oz/1½ cups	water
2 pinches	of salt
1 tablespoon	lime juice
255 g/9 oz/1½ cups	thickly sliced just ripe bananas
400-ml/14-oz can	coconut milk, unshaken

1) Dissolve the sugar in the water with a pinch of salt, then bring to the boil and simmer for 3 minutes.

2) Dribble the lime juice over the banana slices, like a salad dressing, then put the bananas into the hot syrup. Cook gently for 3–4 minutes.

3) Open the can of coconut milk without shaking it first and spoon the thick cream off the top into a small pan (save the milk for another dish). Add a pinch of salt and place it over a fairly high heat to reduce slightly. Don't boil it so hard that it separates. Serve on top of the bananas.

Guavas

This is the easiest recipe in the book.

SERVES 2

2 ripe guavas
1 lemon or lime
   a little sugar

1) Slice the guavas in half, lengthwise.
2) Sprinkle a squeeze of lemon or lime and sugar to taste over the cut surface.

To eat a guava, scoop out the flesh with a teaspoon, like you would an avocado. Eat the softly grainy flesh and the flattish crunchy seeds.

Nam Malakaw Pon

Nam pon is like a fruit milkshake without the milk. Some stalls in the night markets sell only fruit drinks. This one is made with ripe papaya, but you can use the same method with mango, banana, pineapple, peaches, whatever you fancy. Also, instead of water, you can add thinned coconut milk. If you don't care for the Thai addition of salt, just leave it out. A word of caution: you must have a blender that is sufficiently powerful to deal with ice cubes – don't burn out the motor of a weedier one.

SERVES 4–6

1	ripe papaya, peeled, deseeded and cut into chunks
8	ice cubes
125 ml/4½ fl oz/½ cup	water
½ teaspoon	salt
2 teaspoons	sugar
1 teaspoon	lime juice
	fresh mint leaves, to decorate, optional

1) Place everything in the blender, except the mint leaves. Whizz until smooth.
2) Strain into a glass jug and top with a sprig of mint, if using.

Lime Squash

This will become a favourite, especially in the summer. It is also good as a mixer – Thais add a splash of Mekong whisky, but you could try Bourbon or vodka.

SERVES 4–6

a small piece	of root ginger, optional
115 g/4 oz/½ cup	palm or light brown sugar
1 litre/1¾ pints/4 cups	water
2	limes
	fresh mint leaves, to decorate, optional

1) Bruise the ginger, if using, and put it into a small pan with the sugar and 125 ml/5 fl oz/½ cup of the water.
2) Stir over a low heat until the sugar dissolves. Bring to a brisk boil for 2 minutes, then strain the syrup onto the limes in a blender or liquidizer. Add the rest of the water and whizz for 30 seconds on high speed. Strain into a jug and serve cold, decorated with the mint leaves, if using.

Ginger Tea

Ginger Tea is a popular drink in Thailand. It is available freeze-dried, like coffee granules, but it is easy to make at home and is a good way of using up any root ginger that is looking a little old and tired. This tea is reputed to be good for the digestion, headaches and the blood – it is certainly very refreshing.

SERVES 4–6

about 50-g/2-oz piece of root ginger
570 ml/1 pint/2½ cups water
sugar, to taste

1) Bruise the ginger by hitting it a few times with a rolling pin or steak hammer (at last – a use for one in the vegetarian kitchen!)
2) Put into a pan with the water.
3) Simmer for about 10 minutes, until the water turns brown. Strain into a jug and sweeten to taste. Serve hot or well chilled, with or without a slice of lime. Don't throw the ginger out, you can boil it up again with fresh water.

Tamarind Squash

Tamarind Squash has a lovely sweet and sour flavour – so refreshing on a hot day. You must use tamarind paste for this, not the commercially available bottled tamarind purée.

SERVES 4–6

125 g/4½ oz/½ cup	tamarind paste
125 ml/4½ fl oz/½ cup	water
200 g/7 oz/1 cup	sugar
	iced water, to serve

1) Put the tamarind paste, water and sugar into a small pan.
2) Stir over a low heat until the sugar has dissolved. Simmer for about 8–10 minutes, until the mixture is thick.
3) Spoon into a sieve (strainer) and push it through (tamarind pastes often claim they are seedless, but I have never found one that is). Transfer the tamarind mixture to a clean, screw-topped jar and it will keep for up to 2 weeks.
4) To serve, add 1 tablespoon of the tamarind mixture (it is the consistency of malt extract) to a glass of iced water and stir well.

Cooks' Note
You can make tamarind ice lollies (frozen suckers) from not too diluted squash.

Green Papayas

You can buy beautifully prepared green papayas from street vendors in Thailand, complete with a little bag of pinkish powder to dip it in. All the Thai flavours – sour, sweet, hot and salty – are here. It is lovely as a first course or just a snack.

SERVES 4–6

2	green papayas
2 tablespoons	caster (granulated) sugar
1 tablespoon	salt
1 teaspoon	coarsely ground chilli powder

1) Peel the papayas with a vegetable peeler.
2) Slice in half lengthwise and scrape out the seeds.
3) Cut into long thin slices and arrange, fanlike, on plates.
4) Mix together the sugar, salt and chilli powder (the easiest way to do this is to shake them together in a jar or bag). Divide the mixture between the plates, making a little mound on each. Serve.

Banana Chips

These are every bit as moreish as tortilla chips. Thais seldom use bananas in savoury dishes as their neighbours in South-East Asia do. This snack dish is about as far as it goes. But they are very keen on them in desserts and grow nearly 30 different varieties!

SERVES 4–6

vegetable oil, for deep-frying

4 large plantains or green bananas, peeled and thinly sliced

1–2 teaspoons ground dried red chilli

good pinch of salt

1) Heat oil in a deep-fat fryer or wok to 185°C/365°F.
2) Fry the plantain or banana slices in batches until crisp and golden. Drain and toss onto kitchen paper.
3) Dust with the chilli and salt.

Khun Pip's Appetizer

Khun Pip, Director and Teacher at the Thai House Cookery School, gave me the recipe for this simple but delicious nibble to serve with drinks.

SERVES 4–6

1	very fresh lemongrass stem
2	Kaffir lime leaves
125 g/4 oz/scant cup	freshly roasted cashews
2 pinches	of salt
a pinch	of ground chilli, if desired

1) Peel the outer leaves of the lemongrass off and discard. Slice diagonally, upwards from the base, as thinly as you can. When the purple rings in the centre stop, cut only 3 more slices (save the remainder for soup or similar).
2) Put the lime leaves one on top of the other, then roll up tightly, like a cigar. Slice across as thinly as possible.
3) Mix everything together and serve.

Finishing Touches

Finishing touches make a big difference to the look of a dish. They also contribute to the flavours. In the 30-minute timescale there is no room for intricate vegetable carving, but try the following ideas when you've got a moment in hand.

Chilli Flowers
Make 2 to 4 cuts lengthwise from the tip of a long fresh chilli to just before the base. Put it in cold water and the 'petals' will curl back.

Spring Onion (Scallion) Flowers and Frills
Trim the root end neatly. Cut off the other end to leave you with a 5-cm/2-in length. Cut, lengthwise, from just below the root right to the end all the way through. Roll it along until the uncut side is uppermost and repeat. This cut will be at 90 degrees to the first. Place in iced water and the different layers will peel back, looking like the many petals of a flower.

For frills, cut 7.5-cm/3-in lengths of spring onion (scallion) and cut into the middle from both ends in the same way as for flowers, but leave the central 5-mm/¼-in section uncut. Place in iced water and the layers will peel back from each end.

Garlic Flowers
Simply cut pickled garlic horizontally.

Deep-fried Basil Leaves
Drop basil leaves into hot oil and quickly lift them out again and drain on kitchen paper. The noise is quite explosive and they take no time at all. Watch out for spatters.

Index